The Happiness Formula

A Practical Guide to Unlocking Your True Happiness Potential

Christine Michaelis

Copyright © 05.03.2023 Christine Michaelis

All rights reserved. No part of this book may be reproduced, stored in a retrieval system, or transmitted, in any form or by any means, electronic, mechanical, photocopying, recording or otherwise, without the prior written permission of the copyright owner.

ISBN: 9798393657048

Endorsements

"In her book "Happiness Formula," Christine perfectly combines and explains happiness's social, scientific, and practical pillars. Through her thorough and expansive knowledge on the subject, we are guided to awareness of what happens in our brains and bodies when we feel true gratitude, contentment, and joy, allowing all readers to understand why the information is essential in making changes towards a more fulfilling life. On top of this, the thought-provoking questions challenge the readers to put into practice all the information which makes the reading truly transformative. This is a must-read for anybody looking to curate more happiness and genuine joy in their lives. It will be on the top of my gift-giving list from now on."
Corie Wightlin, Wightlin Coaching Services,
https://wightlincoachingservices.com

"The complexity of happiness is simplified with a marvelous formula that instantly made me SMILE =) Christine makes it easy, offering well-documented information and accessible tools for everybody. Along the book, she also proposes insightful questions to reflect about what each scientific statement means to you, giving the chance to pause, take a breath, and integrate the new learnings and understandings. Mindfully written, thought-provoking and empowering".
Ana Rodríguez Rejón, PhD in Human Nutrition, Mindfulness and Emotional Intelligence trainer

This is a great book for anyone wanting more happiness in their life, and let's be honest, who doesn't want to be happier?

I love how Christine has created a straight forward formula that we can all use to enable us to achieve greater happiness. The simple step-by-step approach gives us a framework which we can apply in our everyday lives.

She weaves together a number of different methodologies and theories to provide a comprehensive view on happiness and how to have more of it! I love the questions that she asks throughout the book – a useful prompt to reflect on our own lives and happiness. She gives us tools and provides us with the choice to think differently.

The book is simple yet powerful – apply what you learn and you will become happier.

Emma McNally MBA, NLP Trainer, author and coach www.achieveyourgreatness.co.uk

Dedication

I am dedicating the book to the love of my life Nicolò who accepts me as I am, supports and encourages me every step of my way and makes me happy. Thank you, I love you.

Content

Introduction	6
Acknowledgements	8
What it is all about	9
How to use this book	12
Start Your Journey	14
Make Sure You're Ready	80
Implant Happiness into Your Brain	115
Learn About the Models	203
Engage with Tools	221
A final word	263
About Christine	264
Notes	266

Introduction

Thank you for choosing to purchase this book. By doing so, you have taken an important step towards unlocking the secret to a **happier**, more fulfilling **life**.

Perhaps you picked up this book because you're feeling **stuck**, **dissatisfied**, or **unfulfilled**. Maybe you've been searching for answers to questions like: What is **happiness**? How can I be **happier**? Is there a formula for happiness?

As someone who has spent years exploring these very questions, I can tell you that there is no one solution fits all - BUT there is a **formula for happiness** that can help you to find out what works for you, and it's my hope that this book will help you discover it.

After reading **countless books** on the subject of happiness and joy, as well as completing a **certification** as a **happiness facilitator** from the Museum of Happiness and a course at **Yale University** about the **science of wellbeing**, I have distilled the most valuable insights and wisdom into this book.

In these pages, you'll find a comprehensive guide to the **factors** that **contribute** to **happiness** and how to cultivate them in your own life. Whether you're looking to improve your relationships, boost your sense of purpose, or simply find more joy in everyday moments, you'll find practical strategies and exercises to help you get there.

So without further ado, let's dive in and discover the Happiness Formula together.

Acknowledgements

Dear Family and Nicolò (the love of my life),

As I reflect on my life and the journey that has led me to this point, I am filled with immense gratitude for the love and support that you have provided me. Your unwavering encouragement and belief in me have been instrumental in bringing happiness and fulfillment into my life.

To my family, thank you for always standing by my side and supporting my decisions, even when they may have seemed unconventional or risky. Your love has been a constant source of strength and motivation, and I am truly blessed to have such a loving and supportive family.

And to Nicolò, you are the sunshine in my life, bringing joy and happiness to every moment we spend together. Your unwavering support and unwavering love have given me the courage to pursue my dreams and to be the best version of myself. I am forever grateful for your presence in my life, and I cherish every moment we spend together.

To both my family and my love, you have been my rock and my support system, and I cannot thank you enough for the happiness you have brought into my life. You have shown me what true love and support are, and I am forever grateful for you.

With love and gratitude,

Christine

What it is all about

SMILE Your Way to Happiness

Have you ever wondered what it takes to be truly happy? In this book, we'll explore a **formula** for happiness that is easy to remember and simple to implement. That formula is **SMILE**, which stands for:

S = **Start** Your Journey
M = Make Sure You're **Ready**
I = **Implant** Happiness into Your Brain
L = Learn About the **Models**
E = Engage with **Tools**

Let's take a closer look at each step of the SMILE formula and how it can help you achieve greater happiness and fulfillment in your life.

Step 1: Start Your Journey

- **Understanding** Happiness: What is happiness and why does it matter?
- **Know yourself**: Exploring your personal values, strengths, and purpose
- **Mindfulness**: Techniques for being present and aware in the moment

Step 2: Make Sure You're Ready

- **NLP**: Neuro-Linguistic Programming techniques for cultivating a positive mindset
- Overcoming **Obstacles**: Strategies for overcoming fear, doubt, and negative self-talk
- Setting **Goals**: The power of goal-setting and how to set achievable goals

Step 3: Implant happiness into your brain

- The **Science** of Happiness: Scientific research about what makes people happy
- The **Biology** of Happiness: What happens in our body when we're happy and how to cultivate a healthy mind-body connection
- Building **Habits**: Strategies for creating healthy habits that lead to happiness

Step 4: Learn About the Models

- **PERMA** Model: Understanding the five elements of wellbeing - Positive Emotion, Engagement, Relationships, Meaning, and Accomplishment
- Other **Models**: Exploring other models of happiness, including the Three Circles Model and the Hedonic-Treadmill Model

Step 5: Engage with Tools

- **Gratitude**: The power of gratitude and how to cultivate a grateful mindset
- **Meditation**: Techniques for meditation and mindfulness
- Positive **Affirmations**: Using positive affirmations to cultivate a positive mindset
- **Visualization**: The power of visualization and how to use it to achieve your goals

By following the **SMILE acronym** and implementing the strategies and tools outlined in this book, you'll be well on your way to a happier, more fulfilling life.

How to use this book

This book is packed with **questions, exercises**, and **tools** to help you implement the Happiness Formula using the acronym SMILE.

You can use this book in a few different ways. Some readers prefer to **read through the entire book first**, taking notes and highlighting key points along the way. Then, they go back and work through the exercises and tools section by section, applying the concepts they've learned to their own lives.

Others prefer **to work through the book bit by bit**, completing the exercises and tools as they go along. This can help you stay focused and engaged with the material, and may be particularly helpful if you're short on time or easily distracted.

Whichever approach you choose, it's important to approach this book with an **open mind** and a willingness to **experiment** with new ideas and strategies. Remember, cultivating greater happiness and fulfillment is a journey, and there is **no one-size-fits-all approach**. Take what works for you and leave the rest.

As you work through the exercises and tools in this book, don't be afraid to ask for help or support if you need it. You may want to **share your journey** with a trusted friend or family member, or seek out the guidance of a coach or other professional.

Ultimately, the key to success with this book is to be **consistent** and **persistent**. Keep practicing the strategies and tools outlined in these pages, and over time, you'll begin to notice **a shift in your mood, outlook, and overall wellbeing.**

In the "The Happiness Formula" book, you will find various **exercises** and **questions** designed to help you **reflect** on your life, values, and goals. Some of these questions may be repeated throughout the book, and this is intentional. Repetition is essential for embedding the concepts and ideas presented in the book into your mind and daily life. By asking similar questions in different contexts, the book aims to help you deepen your understanding and apply the insights to various areas of your life. Therefore, don't be surprised if you encounter similar questions or exercises multiple times. Each repetition offers a chance to dive deeper into your thoughts, feelings, and behaviors, and to cultivate self-awareness, which is a critical ingredient for happiness.

You can find additional resources on this page: **www.creativestartupacademy.com/resources-hf**

I also mention the link in the book when I am referring to a resource on the page.

Start Your Journey

Start your journey

As mentioned before, we start with the **S in SMILE - Start your journey**. It is all about understanding yourself better and **understanding** what happiness actually is.

The first thing to understand is that happiness means **different things to different people**. There is not just one way to look at it.

Interpreting the world through a lens of happiness is a powerful tool, as it allows us to **adjust** our perspective even when we are unable to alter our surroundings. By choosing to shift our outlook, we can always find a way to **improve** our relationship with the world around us. Let's look at some concepts around happiness.

The difference between happiness and joy

Happiness and joy are often used interchangeably, but they are distinct emotional states with **subtle differences**. **Happiness** is generally considered to be a **more long-term state of being**, characterized by a deep sense of contentment, satisfaction, and fulfillment. It is often associated with a sense of **purpose** or meaning in life, and is influenced by factors such as personal **values**, **relationships**, and **accomplishments**.

Joy, on the other hand, is generally considered to be a more **fleeting and intense emotion**, often associated with a particular event or experience. It is characterized by feelings of **elation, excitement, and delight**, and can be brought on by a range of experiences, such as achieving a goal, spending time with loved ones, or experiencing the beauty of nature.

While happiness and joy are distinct emotional states, they are not mutually exclusive. In fact, experiencing moments of joy can contribute to overall happiness and wellbeing by providing a sense of pleasure, fulfillment, and positive emotions. Cultivating a sense of happiness, on the other hand, can help to sustain a more **enduring sense** of joy and contentment in life.

In summary, while happiness and joy are distinct emotional states with subtle differences, they both contribute to overall wellbeing and can be cultivated through **intentional practices such as gratitude, mindfulness**, and cultivating **positive relationships**.

Here are some questions you can ask yourself to help understand the difference between happiness and joy:

What does happiness mean to me?

What does joy mean to me?

How do I feel when I'm happy?

How do I feel when I'm joyful?

Are there any specific situations or experiences that make me feel happy?

Are there any specific situations or experiences that make me feel joyful?

How long does happiness typically last for me?

How long does joy typically last for me?

Do I think of happiness as a state of being, or a fleeting emotion?

Do I think of joy as a state of being, or a fleeting emotion?

Reflecting on these questions can help you gain a better understanding of the difference between happiness and joy, and how they manifest in your own life. Remember, there is no right or wrong answer - everyone's experience of happiness and joy is unique.

Pleasure and happiness

In our pursuit of happiness, we often **mistake pleasure for true happiness**. Pleasure is **a fleeting sensation** that arises from **external stimuli**, such as good food, a comfortable bed, or a pleasant experience. It is a physical sensation that is short-lived and dependent on external factors.

True happiness, on the other hand, is a state of being that arises from within, and is not dependent on external factors. It is a deep sense of contentment and inner peace that arises from living a meaningful and fulfilling life.

The problem with pleasure is that it **can be addictive**, and we can become attached to the external stimuli that bring us pleasure. This attachment can lead to negative mental states such as **greed, pride, and envy**, which are incompatible with true happiness.

For example, a person who is addicted to the pleasure of shopping may experience a temporary sense of happiness when they make a new purchase. However, this pleasure is often accompanied by feelings of pride or superiority, which can lead to negative consequences such as overspending, debt, or a distorted sense of self-worth.

In contrast, true happiness arises **from living a life of purpose and meaning**. It is a deep sense of contentment that comes from cultivating positive mental states such as kindness, compassion, and generosity. When we live in alignment with our values and focus on the well-being of others, we experience a sense of fulfillment and purpose that cannot be found in external pleasures.

In summary, pleasure can be a fleeting sensation that is often accompanied by negative mental states, while true **happiness is a state of being that arises from within and is not dependent on external factors**.

Definition of happiness by Matthieu Ricard

"Happiness and wellbeing is not just a pleasurable sensation, it is a **deep sense of serenity and fulfillment**. A state that **underlies** all emotional states and all the joys and sorrows that can comes one's way" - Matthieu Ricard

Matthieu Ricard, a renowned **Buddhist monk** and author, offers a thought-provoking definition of happiness. He suggests that happiness and wellbeing are not just fleeting pleasurable sensations, but rather a deep sense of serenity and fulfillment that underlies all emotional states.

This definition speaks to the idea that happiness is **not just about experiencing positive emotions or avoiding negative ones**, but about cultivating a sense of **inner peace and contentment** that remains steady even amidst life's ups and downs. Ricard's definition suggests that true happiness is not dependent on external circumstances, but rather on cultivating an inner state of being that is **resilient**, **peaceful**, and **fulfilled**. By viewing happiness in this way, we can cultivate a more enduring sense of joy and wellbeing that is not easily shaken by the challenges and uncertainties of life.

Happiness in buddhism

Chogyam Trungpa was a **Tibetan master** who emphasized the importance of **mindfulness** and **self-awareness in achieving inner peace and enlightenment**. One of the key concepts in his teachings is the **idea of ignorance**, which he viewed as a fundamental obstacle to spiritual growth.

According to Trungpa, ignorance is not simply a lack of knowledge or understanding, but rather a **willful blindness to the true nature of reality**. It is a form of delusion that prevents us from seeing the world as it truly is, and from recognizing the interconnectedness of all things.

Trungpa believed that ignorance was the **root of many of the problems** we face in the world today, including greed, aggression, and environmental destruction. He taught that by cultivating awareness and mindfulness, we can begin to overcome our ignorance and develop a deeper understanding of ourselves and the world around us.

In Trungpa's teachings, **happiness and enlightenment** are not seen as something that can be achieved through external means, but rather as a **state of being that arises naturally** when we let go of our illusions and embrace the truth of our

interconnectedness with all things. By recognizing our own ignorance and actively working to overcome it, we can begin to move towards a more authentic and fulfilling life.

The concept of cause and effect is a central tenet of Buddhism, and it governs both happiness and suffering. According to this principle, **every action we take has consequences**, and these consequences can either lead to happiness or suffering.

In Buddhism, the law of cause and effect is known as **karma**. Karma is not seen as a punishment or reward, but rather as a natural law that governs the workings of the universe. Every thought, word, and action we take creates an imprint on our consciousness, and these imprints determine the course of our lives.

Positive actions create positive karma, which leads to happiness and well-being. Negative actions create negative karma, which leads to suffering and pain. However, the effects of our actions are not always immediate or obvious. Sometimes the consequences of our actions may not **manifest until a later time, or in a different form than we expect**.

In Buddhism, the goal is to **cultivate positive karma** through **ethical conduct, meditation, and wisdom**. By living a life of **kindness**, **generosity**, and **compassion**, we create positive imprints on our consciousness that lead to happiness and well-being. By **cultivating wisdom** and insight, we gain a deeper **understanding** of the **nature** of reality and the **interdependence** of all things.

Ultimately, the law of cause and effect reminds us that **we are not separate from the world around us**, and that our actions have a profound impact on ourselves and others.

The Buddhist concept of **impermanence** teaches us that everything is constantly changing at every moment. Nothing in this world is permanent, and everything is in a **constant state of flux**. This includes our thoughts, emotions, and physical sensations.

At first glance, the idea of **impermanence** might seem bleak and depressing. However, it can actually be a source of **great joy and liberation**. When we realize that everything is impermanent, we are **liberated from attachment** and **clinging** to things that cannot provide lasting happiness.

Happiness is often associated with clinging to pleasant experiences and trying to avoid unpleasant ones. However, the truth is that all experiences, pleasant or unpleasant, are impermanent and fleeting. When we recognize the impermanent nature of all things, we are less likely to cling to them and more likely to **appreciate** them for what they are in **the moment**.

Furthermore, the **impermanence** of all things can be a source of **inspiration** and **motivation**. It reminds us that we have the power to change our lives and create new experiences. When we recognize that everything is impermanent, we are encouraged to **make the most of the present moment** and live our lives to the fullest.

In summary, the concept of impermanence teaches us that everything is constantly changing at every moment. While this may seem unsettling at first, it can actually be a source of great joy and liberation. When we recognize the impermanent nature of all things, we are liberated from attachment and clinging, and are more likely to appreciate the present moment for what it is.

Ubuntu

The concept of **ubuntu**, which comes from the **Bantu** languages of **Southern Africa**, emphasizes the **interconnectedness** and **interdependence of all beings.** It is a philosophy that recognizes that we are all part of a larger community, and that our **happiness** is intimately **connected** with the **happiness of others**.

In the Ubuntu philosophy, happiness is not seen as an individual pursuit, but rather as a **collective goal**. The well-being of each individual is seen as vital to the well-being of the whole community, and the community has a responsibility to ensure that each individual is able to thrive and flourish.

Ubuntu emphasizes the **importance of empathy**, **compassion**, and understanding in promoting happiness and well-being. When we recognize our shared humanity and the interdependence of all beings, we are more likely to **act in ways that promote the happiness and well-being of others**.

Ubuntu also emphasizes the importance of a sense of belonging and connection to others. When we feel connected to our community and have a sense of **purpose and belonging**, we are more likely to experience happiness and fulfillment in our lives.

In summary, the concept of ubuntu emphasizes the interconnectedness and interdependence of all beings, and recognizes that our happiness is intimately connected with the happiness of others. By promoting empathy, compassion, and a sense of belonging, ubuntu can help to create a more harmonious and fulfilling society where everyone can thrive and flourish.

The 2 dimensions of happiness

There are **two dimensions** of happiness that have been extensively researched in the field of psychology: **hedonic and eudaimonic happiness**.

Hedonic happiness

Hedonic happiness refers to the **experience of pleasure** and the **absence of pain**. It is often associated with the pursuit of happiness through the fulfillment of desires and the avoidance of negative emotions. This dimension of happiness is focused on seeking out experiences and activities that are **pleasurable, enjoyable, and fun**. Examples of hedonic activities might include **watching a movie**, going out for a nice **meal**, or engaging in a favorite **hobby**.

Eudaimonic happiness

Eudaimonic happiness, on the other hand, refers to a **deeper sense of wellbeing and fulfillment** that comes from living a life of purpose and meaning. This dimension of happiness is focused on cultivating **positive relationships**, pursuing meaningful **goals**, and engaging in activities that align with one's personal **values** and sense of **purpose**. Examples of eudaimonic activities might include **volunteering** for a cause you care about, pursuing a **challenging career**

path, or engaging in **personal growth** and **development**.

While both dimensions of happiness are important for overall wellbeing, research suggests that **eudaimonic** happiness may be more closely linked to **long-term wellbeing and life satisfaction**. Pursuing a life of purpose and meaning, cultivating positive relationships, and engaging in activities that align with one's personal values can help to foster **a deeper sense of fulfillment** and wellbeing that extends beyond momentary pleasure or the avoidance of negative emotions.

In summary, while hedonic and eudaimonic happiness are distinct dimensions of happiness, they both play important roles in overall wellbeing.

Here are some questions you can ask yourself to help understand the difference between hedonic happiness and eudaimonic happiness:

What is my definition of hedonic happiness?

What is my definition of eudaimonic happiness?

When have I experienced hedonic happiness?

What was the situation or experience that made me feel that way?

When have I experienced eudaimonic happiness?

What was the situation or experience that made me feel that way?

How do I feel when I pursue activities that bring me hedonic happiness?

How do I feel when I pursue activities that bring me eudaimonic happiness?

Do I believe that pleasure or satisfaction is the key to happiness, or do I believe that living a meaningful life is the key to happiness?

What are some examples of hedonic activities or experiences that I enjoy?

What are some examples of eudaimonic activities or experiences that I enjoy?

How do I balance my pursuit of hedonic happiness and eudaimonic happiness in my daily life?

Do I believe that one type of happiness is more important or valuable than the other? Why or why not?

How do I prioritize my values and goals when it comes to achieving happiness?

What role do relationships, connections, and social support play in my experience of hedonic and eudaimonic happiness?

Reflecting on these questions can help you gain a deeper understanding of the differences between hedonic and eudaimonic happiness, and how they apply to your own life and values.

The happiness chemicals

To look at some chemical reactions and the 'happiness chemicals' you can use the acronym **DOSE - Dopamine, Oxytocin, Serotonin, Endorphins**

Dopamine, oxytocin, serotonin, and endorphins are four **chemicals** in the brain that are often associated with happiness and wellbeing. Each of these chemicals plays a unique role in the brain and **is released under different circumstances.**

Dopamine

Dopamine is often called the **"reward" chemical**, and is released when we **experience** something **pleasurable** or **rewarding**. It is associated with feelings of pleasure and motivation, and is often released in response to things like food, sex, or accomplishing a goal. When we achieve something that we've been working towards, dopamine is released, which can create a **sense of satisfaction and fulfillment**.

Oxytocin

Oxytocin is often called the **"bonding" chemical**, and is released when we engage in **social interactions** and build positive relationships with others. It is associated with feelings of trust, empathy, and connection, and is often released in response to things like **physical touch**, **socializing**, or engaging in acts of **kindness**.

Serotonin

Serotonin is often called the "**mood stabilizer**" **chemical**, and is involved in **regulating mood, sleep, and appetite**. It is associated with feelings of calm, contentment, and well-being, and is often released in response to things like **exercise**, exposure to **sunlight**, or engaging in activities that promote **relaxation**.

Endorphins

Endorphins are often called the "**painkiller**" **chemicals**, and are released in response **to physical exertion or stress**. They are associated with feelings of pleasure and can help to **reduce feelings of pain and stress**. Endorphins are often released in response to things like **exercise**, **laughter**, or engaging in activities that **require mental focus**.

In summary, these four chemicals play a crucial role in the brain's **regulation of mood, wellbeing, and happiness**. By **engaging in activities** that promote the release of these chemicals, such as exercise, socializing, or pursuing meaningful goals, we can **cultivate a greater sense of wellbeing and happiness** in our lives. Additionally, practices like mindfulness, meditation, and gratitude can help to promote the release of these chemicals and support overall wellbeing.

Where happiness comes from

According to **Sonja Lyubomirsky**, a professor of psychology at the University of California, Riverside, happiness is influenced by **three main factors**: genetics, actions and thoughts, and life circumstances.

Lyubomirsky's research suggests that **genetics** plays a significant role in determining our baseline level of happiness, accounting for approximately **50% of our overall happiness**. This means that some individuals may have a predisposition towards being happier or less happy based on their genetic makeup.

However, Lyubomirsky's research also suggests that our actions and thoughts play a significant role in determining our level of happiness. Specifically, she suggests **that intentional behaviors and thoughts** such as practicing gratitude, engaging in acts of kindness, and focusing on positive experiences can increase our overall happiness. This factor is estimated to account for approximately **40% of our overall happiness.**

Finally, Lyubomirsky suggests that **life circumstances - such as income, social status, and relationships** - account for only approximately **10% of our overall happiness.** While these factors may have some influence on our happiness in the short term, their impact tends to be temporary and fleeting.

Overall, Lyubomirsky's research suggests that while genetics may play a significant role in determining our baseline level of happiness, our intentional behaviors and thoughts play a larger role in determining our overall happiness. By cultivating positive habits and focusing on the things that bring us joy and fulfillment, we can increase our overall happiness and wellbeing, regardless of our life circumstances.

Here are some questions you can ask yourself based on the three factors that influence happiness, according to Sonja Lyubomirsky:

Genetics

Do I believe that my level of happiness is largely determined by my genetics?

Are there specific traits or tendencies that run in my family that could impact my happiness?

How do I react to situations that challenge my happiness? Do I tend to bounce back quickly, or do I struggle to recover?

Am I generally an optimistic or pessimistic person? How does this impact my happiness?

Do I believe that I have the power to overcome any genetic predisposition towards unhappiness?

Actions and thoughts

What actions or behaviors make me feel happy or fulfilled?

What thoughts or beliefs do I have that contribute to my happiness or unhappiness?

Am I actively seeking out opportunities for joy and fulfillment, or am I waiting for happiness to come to me?

How do I handle setbacks or failures? Do I tend to dwell on negative events, or do I focus on moving forward? How do my daily habits and routines impact my overall level of happiness?

Life circumstances:

What major life events or circumstances have contributed to my happiness or unhappiness in the past?

Am I currently experiencing any major life changes or challenges that could impact my happiness?

How do my relationships with others impact my happiness? Are there any relationships that could be improved to boost my overall well-being?

How do I feel about my career or work life? Does my job bring me fulfillment and happiness?

How do I feel about my financial situation? Does money play a role in my overall level of happiness?

Reflecting on these questions can help you gain a better understanding of the factors that influence your happiness, and help you identify areas for growth and improvement. Remember, happiness is a complex and multifaceted experience, and it's important to approach it with curiosity, self-compassion, and a willingness to learn and grow.

Synthetic and natural happiness

According to social psychologist **Dan Gilbert**, there are **two types of happiness: synthetic and natural.**

Synthetic happiness is the happiness we **create for ourselves** when we **don't get something** we want or when we settle for something less than what we desire.

On the other hand, **natural happiness** is the joy we experience when **we get what we want or desire**.

Gilbert's research shows that both types of happiness **are equally powerful** and can lead **to long-term happiness.** Many people mistakenly believe that natural happiness is better and more satisfying than synthetic happiness. However, Gilbert's research suggests otherwise. He found that people who created synthetic happiness were just as happy and satisfied as those who experienced natural happiness.

Moreover, Gilbert's research shows that **people are actually quite good at synthesizing happiness**. When people can't change a situation, they often change the way they think about it. They focus on the positive aspects of the situation and find reasons to be happy with what they have.

In conclusion, synthetic happiness is just as important as natural happiness. Building the habit of creating synthetic happiness can help you maintain a **positive attitude** and **find joy in any situation**. By learning to find the positive in difficult situations and creating your own happiness, you can increase your overall level of happiness and life satisfaction.

Here are some questions one might ask oneself with regards to synthetic and natural happiness:

What is synthetic happiness, and how is it different from natural happiness?

Can synthetic happiness be as fulfilling and long-lasting as natural happiness?

How do I know if the happiness I'm feeling is natural or synthetic?

Am I pursuing goals and experiences that align with my values and bring me natural happiness, or am I chasing synthetic happiness through external validation or material possessions?

Do I believe that I can create my own happiness, or do I feel like my happiness is largely determined by external factors?

Have there been times when I've pursued synthetic happiness and found it to be unsatisfying or fleeting?

Am I willing to prioritize my natural happiness over short-term pleasures or temporary sources of synthetic happiness?

Do I have a healthy balance between pursuing goals and enjoying the present moment, which can bring both natural and synthetic happiness?

How can I cultivate more natural happiness in my life, such as through cultivating gratitude, nurturing relationships, or engaging in activities that bring me joy?

Am I willing to let go of beliefs or habits that may be blocking my natural happiness, such as negative self-talk or a focus on external validation?

Our annoying features of the mind

Our **minds** are **complex** and **powerful tools**, but they also come with their own set of **annoying features** that can sometimes work against us.

Holding onto strong intuitions

The first annoying feature is our **mind's tendency to hold onto strong intuitions that are often wrong**. We may think that achieving a certain goal, acquiring a **certain possession**, or engaging in a particular behavior will make us happy. However, studies have shown that these strong intuitions are often misguided and do not lead to lasting happiness. In fact, the things that actually bring us happiness are often more simple and mundane than we might think, such as spending time with loved ones, engaging in hobbies, or practicing gratitude.

Judging ourselves relative to reference points

The second annoying feature of our mind is our tendency to **judge ourselves and our experiences relative to reference points**. This can take the form of **social comparison**, where we judge our own successes and failures based on where other people are at in their own lives. For example, we may feel inadequate if we don't achieve a certain level of success in our careers by a certain age, simply because we are comparing ourselves to others who have achieved more. This tendency to judge ourselves relative to others can lead to feelings of inadequacy, envy, and frustration.

Happiness is often influenced by how we are doing relative to others

Annoying feature 3 of our mind is that we tend to **compare ourselves to others and our happiness** is often influenced by how we are doing relative to others. It has been observed that people often prefer to earn less if everyone else earns less, rather than earning double but with everyone else earning more. Additionally, when we see celebrities or people with extravagant lifestyles, **our brains don't distinguish between reality and fantasy**.

As a result, the emotional effects we get from seeing these things don't last very long and **we quickly become accustomed** to them. This phenomenon is called **hedonic adaptation**, where **we become less sensitive to positive experiences over time**, and the wonderful things that once brought us joy and happiness become less wonderful with repetition.

Getting used to things

Annoying feature 4 of our mind is that **we tend to get used to things and take them for granted.** This is known as the adaptation level theory, which suggests that we evaluate events and experiences relative to our past experiences, rather than on an absolute scale. As a result, we **often fail to appreciate the good things** in our lives and become accustomed to them. For example, when we get a new job, we may feel happy and excited at first, but over time, we may take it for granted and start to focus on its flaws and challenges. This can lead to a sense of dissatisfaction and a desire for something new and exciting.

To counter these annoying features, it's important to **focus on cultivating gratitude and mindfulness in our daily lives**. By actively practicing gratitude, we can train our minds to appreciate the good things in our lives and avoid taking them for granted. Additionally, by practicing mindfulness, we can learn to be **fully present in the moment** and appreciate the simple pleasures of life. By being aware of these annoying features of our mind, we can work to overcome them and lead happier, more fulfilling lives.

While these annoying features of our minds can be **frustrating**, it's important to **remember that they are natural tendencies** that have evolved over time. By becoming aware of these tendencies and consciously working to overcome them, we can lead happier and more fulfilling lives. This might **involve setting more realistic expectations** for ourselves, practicing mindfulness and gratitude, or consciously focusing on our own goals and desires rather than comparing ourselves to others.

Here are some questions you can ask yourself about the annoying features of the mind mentioned:

Tendency to hold onto strong intuitions

Do I find myself holding onto strong intuitions even when presented with evidence that contradicts them?

How has my tendency to hold onto strong intuitions impacted my decision-making and problem-solving in the past?

What strategies can I use to challenge my intuitions and remain open-minded in my thinking?

Tendency to judge ourselves and our experiences relative to reference points

In what ways do I compare myself to others in my life, whether it's in terms of success, appearance, or other factors?

How do these comparisons impact my self-esteem and overall level of happiness?

What reference points do I use to evaluate my experiences, and how do these impact my perception of success or failure?

Tendency to compare ourselves to others

In what areas of my life do I tend to compare myself to others?

How do these comparisons impact my level of happiness, and in what ways might I be able to shift my focus away from comparison?

What other measures of success or happiness can I focus on instead of external comparison?

Tendency to get used to things and take them for granted

Am I taking the good things in my life for granted?

What are some things in my life that I appreciate but may be getting accustomed to?

Have I been feeling dissatisfied or ungrateful lately?

How can I actively cultivate a sense of appreciation for the good things in my life?

What are some strategies I can use to avoid taking things for granted and maintain a positive outlook on life?

By reflecting on these questions, you can begin to understand how these annoying features of the mind may be impacting your happiness and wellbeing, and develop strategies to overcome them. Remember, it's important to approach these challenges with self-compassion and a willingness to learn and grow.

Miswanting

Miswanting is a common **human experience where we are mistaken about what and how much we will like something in the future**. We often make **decisions based on** our **current desires** and preferences, assuming that they will remain the same in the future. However, research has shown that our **future** desires and preferences can be **difficult to predict**, and we may end up regretting our choices.

For example, we may think that buying a new car or getting a promotion will make us happier in the long run. However, we may be miswanting if we overestimate the impact of these events on our future happiness. In reality, the joy we feel from acquiring something new or achieving a goal may be short-lived, and we may soon return to our previous level of happiness.

Miswanting can also lead us **to engage** in behaviors that are ultimately **harmful to our well-being**, such as overeating, overspending, or engaging in risky behaviors. We may think that these activities will bring us pleasure or excitement, but in the long run, they can lead to negative consequences and feelings of regret.

To **overcome miswanting**, it can be helpful to **take a step back** and reflect on our true desires and goals. Instead of focusing on short-term pleasures or material possessions, we can **focus on cultivating meaningful relationships, engaging in activities that bring us joy and fulfillment, and pursuing our passions and values**.

Here are some questions to help you explore the concept of miswanting:

Have I ever made a decision based on my current desires and preferences, only to regret it later on?

In what situations do I find myself most likely to experience miswanting? Is it related to certain types of decisions or contexts?

How can I improve my ability to predict my future desires and preferences?

Are there any strategies or techniques I can use to make more informed decisions?

Have there been times when I have made a decision that I thought would make me happy, but it didn't?

What can I learn from these experiences?

How can I balance my current desires and preferences with the potential for future change and uncertainty?

Are there any factors I should consider when making decisions that may impact my future happiness?

Am I currently cultivating meaningful relationships with others?

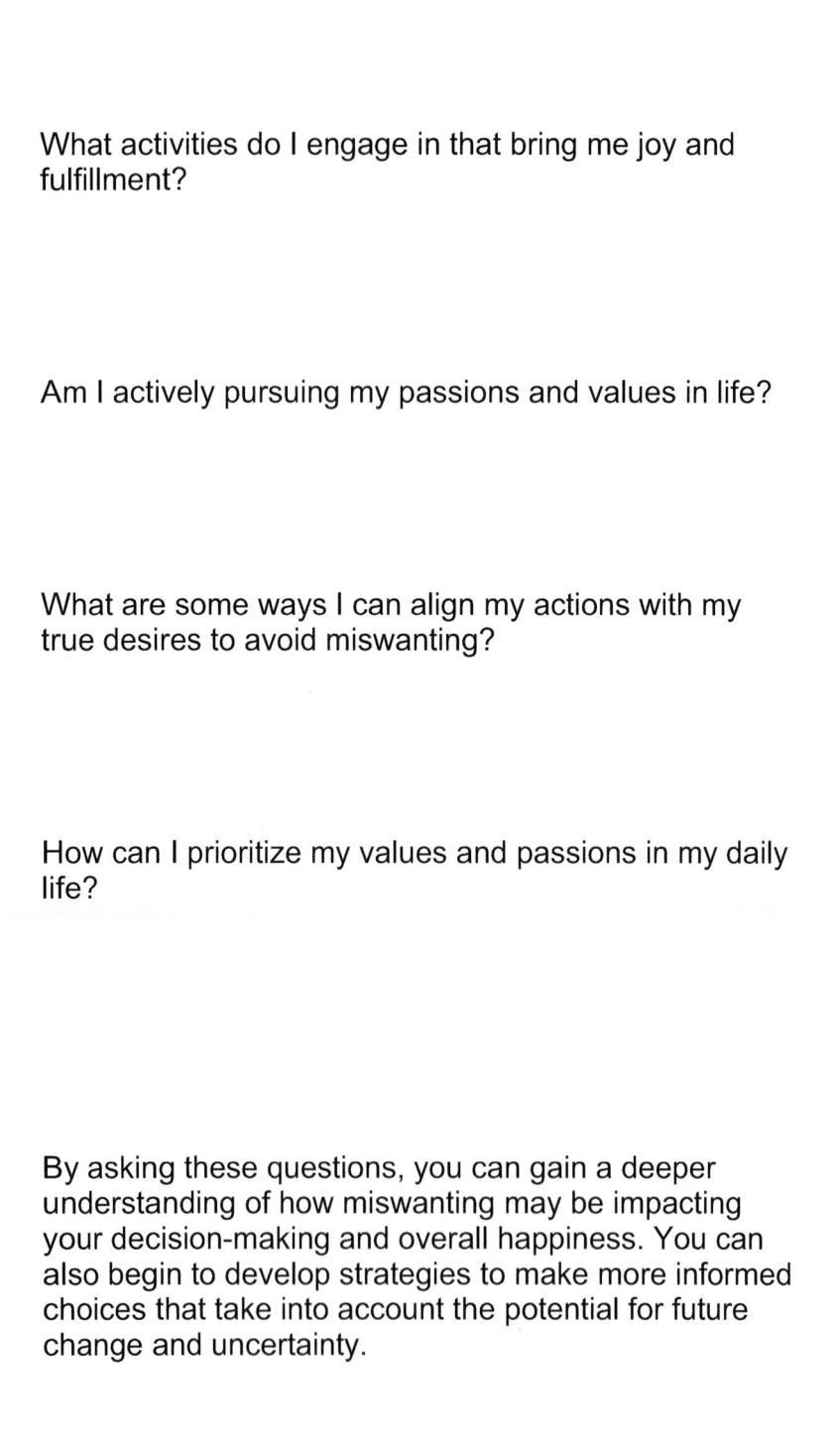

What activities do I engage in that bring me joy and fulfillment?

Am I actively pursuing my passions and values in life?

What are some ways I can align my actions with my true desires to avoid miswanting?

How can I prioritize my values and passions in my daily life?

By asking these questions, you can gain a deeper understanding of how miswanting may be impacting your decision-making and overall happiness. You can also begin to develop strategies to make more informed choices that take into account the potential for future change and uncertainty.

Self compassion/sympathy/empathy

Self-compassion, self-sympathy, and empathy are all related concepts, but there are **important differences** between them. Here's an overview:

Self-compassion

Self-compassion is the practice of being kind, **supportive**, and **understanding towards yourself**, especially during times of difficulty or challenge. Self-compassion involves treating yourself with the same care and compassion that you would extend to a good friend. It means acknowledging your own pain and suffering, and responding with warmth, empathy, and self-care.

Self-sympathy

Self-sympathy is similar to self-compassion, but it **involves feeling sorry for oneself** rather than being kind and supportive. Self-sympathy can involve self-pity, rumination, or dwelling on one's problems without taking action to address them. Unlike self-compassion, self-sympathy can reinforce negative self-talk and feelings of helplessness.

Empathy

Empathy is the ability to **understand and share the feelings of others.** It involves being attuned to the emotions of others, and responding with compassion, care, and support. Empathy involves putting oneself in another person's shoes and imagining how they might be feeling in a given situation.

In summary, while self-compassion and empathy involve treating oneself and others with care and understanding, self-sympathy involves feeling sorry for oneself and can be counterproductive to one's well-being. It's important to cultivate self-compassion and empathy, and to be aware of and avoid falling into patterns of self-sympathy or self-pity.

Here are some questions you can answer to get a better understanding about the topic and yourself:

In what ways do I show compassion to myself when I am going through a difficult time?

How can I cultivate self-compassion in my daily life?

Do I tend to judge myself harshly when I make mistakes?

How can I be more understanding and compassionate towards myself?

What are some examples of self-sympathy in action? How can I practice self-sympathy when I am feeling down or discouraged?

How does empathy differ from self-compassion and self-sympathy?

How can I develop my empathy towards others without neglecting my own self-care?

Do I tend to put others' needs before my own, even at the expense of my own well-being? How can I balance my empathy towards others with self-compassion and self-care?

How can I become more aware of my own emotions and needs, and respond to them with self-compassion and self-sympathy?

What are some practical strategies I can use to cultivate self-compassion, self-sympathy, and empathy in my daily life?

How can I use self-compassion, self-sympathy, and empathy to improve my relationships with others?

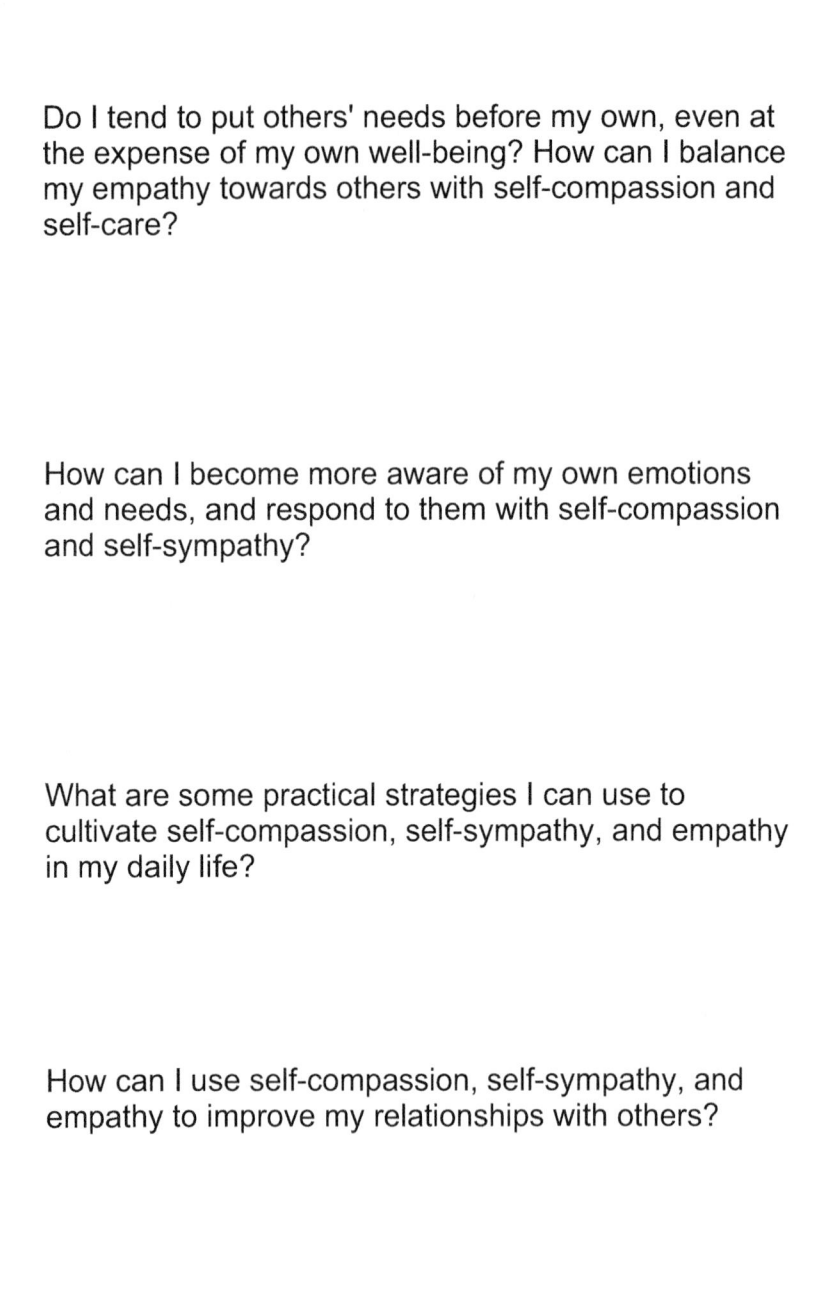

How can I continue to practice self-compassion, self-sympathy, and empathy even when I am feeling stressed or overwhelmed?

Broken vs. stuck

When it comes to happiness, it's important to recognize the difference between feeling broken and feeling stuck.

Feeling broken often stems from a **sense of disappointment or disillusionment with oneself**. You might feel like you're not living up to your own expectations or that you're failing in some way. This can lead to feelings of **sadness**, **hopelessness**, and a **lack of motivation**. When you feel broken, it can be difficult to see a way forward and to find joy in your daily life.

On the other hand, **feeling stuck** is more about feeling **trapped in a situation** or circumstance that you don't know how to change. You might feel like you're in a dead-end job, a toxic relationship, or a negative thought pattern that you can't seem to shake. When you feel stuck, you may feel **frustrated**, **restless**, and **unfulfilled**. You might feel like you're not living up to your potential or that life is passing you by.

While both feelings can be challenging, **it's important to recognize the difference** between the two.

When you **feel broken**, it's important to **practice self-compassion** and focus on building yourself up rather than tearing yourself down. This might involve seeking support from a trusted friend or therapist, practicing self-care, or setting small achievable goals to help rebuild your confidence.

When you **feel stuck**, it's important to **take action** and start making changes to your situation. This might involve taking a new job, ending a toxic relationship, or seeking professional help to break free from negative thought patterns. It can be helpful to set goals and create a plan for how you will achieve them, breaking down big changes into small achievable steps.

Ultimately, finding happiness requires both self-compassion and action.

Answer the following questions:

Do I feel like I am just going through the motions in life, or do I feel like I am completely stuck and unable to make progress towards my goals?

How often do I experience moments of joy or contentment in my life?

Are these moments few and far between, or do they happen frequently?

When I feel unhappy or dissatisfied with my life, do I feel like this is a temporary state that I can overcome, or do I feel like something inside me is fundamentally broken?

How do I respond to setbacks or challenges in my life?

Do I tend to bounce back quickly, or do I get stuck in a negative mindset for long periods of time?

Am I able to find pleasure and enjoyment in simple things, like spending time with loved ones or pursuing hobbies, even when my life isn't going perfectly?

Do I feel like I have a sense of purpose or meaning in my life, even if I am struggling to achieve my goals?

Have I experienced traumatic events or ongoing stressors that might be contributing to my sense of being broken or stuck?

If so, what steps can I take to address these issues?

How can I cultivate a growth mindset that allows me to see setbacks and challenges as opportunities for learning and growth?

What resources and support do I have available to me when I am feeling broken or stuck? Who can I turn to for help and guidance?

How can I practice self-compassion and kindness towards myself, even when I am feeling unhappy or dissatisfied with my life?

Psychological flexibility

Psychological flexibility refers to the ability to **adapt and adjust one's thoughts, emotions, and behaviors in response to changing circumstances.** It involves being open and receptive to different perspectives, as well as being willing to engage in new and different behaviors in pursuit of one's goals and values.

People who are psychologically flexible are often **able to cope with stress and adversity more effectively**, as they are able to shift their attention and focus as needed. They are also more **resilient** and better able to **bounce back** from setbacks, as they are able to see challenges as opportunities for **growth and learning**.

Psychological flexibility is particularly important in the realm of mental health, as it can help individuals manage symptoms of anxiety and depression, improve relationships, and enhance overall well-being. Some ways to cultivate psychological flexibility include:

Practice mindfulness

Mindfulness involves **paying attention to the present** moment without judgment. By practicing mindfulness, individuals can learn to observe their thoughts and emotions without getting caught up in them, which can enhance psychological flexibility.

Clarify your values

Identifying your personal values can **help you make decisions** and take actions that are aligned with your goals and priorities. By staying connected to your values, you can **maintain a sense of purpose and direction**, even in the face of challenges and setbacks.

Develop flexible thinking patterns

Instead of getting stuck in rigid thinking patterns, try to approach situations with a **sense of curiosity and openness**. Consider different perspectives and try to **reframe challenges** as opportunities for growth.

Take small steps

Taking action towards your goals, no matter how small, can help build momentum and enhance psychological flexibility. By trying new things and stepping **outside your comfort zone**, you can cultivate a sense of resilience and adaptability.

Overall, psychological flexibility is a valuable skill that can help individuals thrive in all aspects of their lives.

Here are some questions that you can answer around psychological flexibility:

Am I able to adapt to new situations and challenges, or do I find myself feeling stuck or resistant to change?

Do I tend to avoid difficult emotions or situations, or am I willing to face them head-on and work through them?

How do I respond when things don't go according to plan? Do I become frustrated and give up, or do I look for creative solutions and new opportunities?

How can I become more aware of my thoughts, feelings, and behaviors, and use this awareness to make positive changes in my life?

How can I cultivate a sense of openness and curiosity towards my experiences, even when they are challenging or uncomfortable?

How can I develop my capacity for mindfulness and present-moment awareness, in order to better connect with myself and my surroundings?

Am I able to set goals and work towards them, while remaining flexible and adaptable in the face of changing circumstances?

How can I practice self-compassion and self-acceptance, even when I am struggling or facing difficult emotions?

What steps can I take to build my resilience and bounce back from setbacks or failures?

How can I use my strengths and values to guide my decisions and actions, while remaining open to new opportunities and experiences?

What does Happiness mean to you?

We've explored various concepts of happiness from different cultures, as well as the findings from research and theories. But **what does happiness truly mean to you?** Let's take a closer look.

Finding out what happiness means to oneself is an important journey towards a fulfilling life. It's easy to get caught up in the external factors of our lives, such as our careers or relationships, and forget about what truly brings us joy and happiness. The first step in this journey is to **ask yourself the question, "What does happiness mean to me?"**

Everyone's answer to this question is unique, as happiness is a subjective experience. For some people, happiness may mean spending time with loved ones, while for others, it may mean achieving a career goal or pursuing a passion. Whatever your answer may be, it's important to **take the time to reflect on what truly brings you joy and fulfillment in life.**

One way to do this is to **pay attention to your emotions and feelings** throughout your daily life.

Notice what activities or experiences bring you joy, excitement, or contentment. **Take note** of the things that **drain your energy** or cause stress and **anxiety**. This awareness can help you identify what truly brings you happiness and what may be holding you back from experiencing it.

It's also important to recognize that our definition of happiness **may change over time**. What brought us joy and fulfillment in the past may no longer do so in the present. This is why it's important to **continually reflect** on what happiness means to us and make adjustments as needed.

In conclusion, finding out what happiness means to oneself is a personal and ongoing journey. By taking the time to reflect on our emotions and experiences, we can identify what truly brings us joy and fulfillment in life and make intentional choices that align with our definition of happiness.

By taking the time to reflect on these questions, you can gain a deeper understanding of what truly brings you joy and fulfillment in life and make intentional choices that align with your definition of happiness.

What activities or experiences make me feel truly happy and fulfilled?

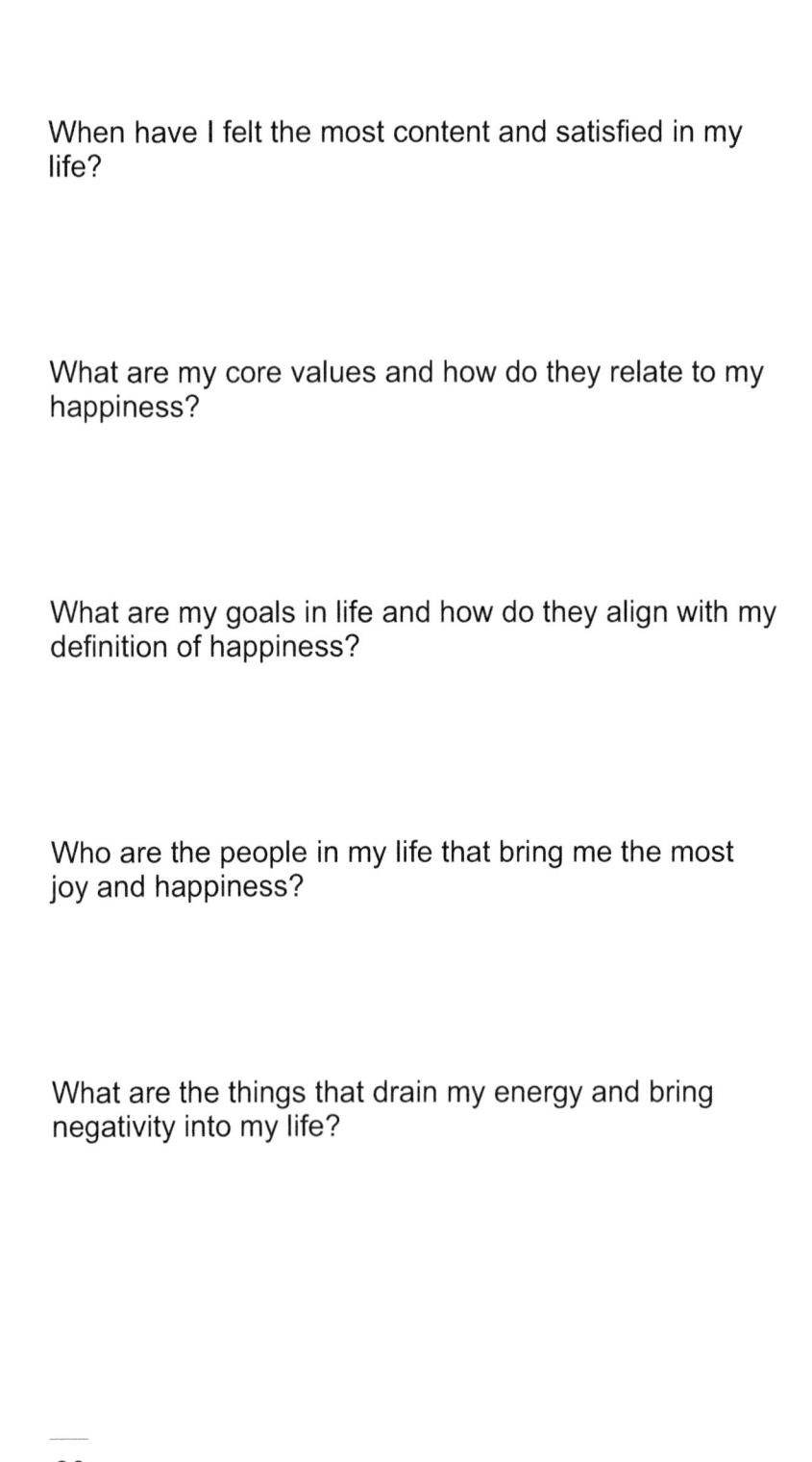

When have I felt the most content and satisfied in my life?

What are my core values and how do they relate to my happiness?

What are my goals in life and how do they align with my definition of happiness?

Who are the people in my life that bring me the most joy and happiness?

What are the things that drain my energy and bring negativity into my life?

How can I limit or eliminate the things that drain my energy or cause stress and anxiety?

How do I define success and does it align with my definition of happiness?

What makes me feel a sense of purpose and meaning in my life?

What are the activities or experiences that bring me a sense of peace and calm?

When I picture my ideal life, what does it look like and how does it make me feel?

How often do I pay attention to my emotions and feelings throughout the day?

What steps can I take to prioritize and focus on the activities that bring me the most happiness and fulfillment?

By exploring your emotions in relation to happiness, you can gain a deeper understanding of how happiness feels and how you can cultivate more of it in your life.

When was the last time I felt truly happy and what was the situation?

What emotions do I associate with happiness (e.g. joy, contentment, excitement, peace)?

How do I know when I am feeling happy?

What are some of the physical sensations I experience when I feel happy (e.g. lightness, warmth, relaxation)?

How does happiness impact my relationships with others?

What role does gratitude play in my experience of happiness?

What are some of the obstacles that prevent me from feeling happy and how can I overcome them?

How do I cope with difficult emotions when they arise and how does this impact my ability to experience happiness?

What are some of the simple pleasures in life that bring me happiness and how can I incorporate more of them into my daily routine?

What are some of the things I can do to cultivate a sense of inner peace and joy in my life?

Your values

Knowing your values is crucial for your happiness because it provides a **clear sense of direction and purpose in life.** When you are aware of your values, you can prioritize your time and energy towards activities and experiences that align with them, and this can bring a sense of fulfillment and satisfaction. Conversely, ignoring your values or living a life that contradicts them can cause feelings of discontentment and a lack of meaning. By identifying and living according to your values, you can create a sense of purpose and direction in life, leading to greater happiness and fulfillment.

What are values?

According to The Oxford English Dictionary: Values are principles of standards of behaviours. **They are one's judgement of what is important in life.**

And another way to define values: They are the basis on which many of our decisions are made and affect our thoughts and actions. They define what you **stand for.**

You can use the exercise that we explain here to discover your personal values.

Defining your values

I will now explain a way to define your values. This might take a moment to get your head around.

Take several **pieces of paper** or post it notes.

Brainstorm your values and write each value on a different piece of paper/post it note. Ask yourself 'What do I value?' 'What is important to me?' and 'What do I want people to feel when they hear my name?' Come up with at least 15 values.

1. Put the values in order of importance to you. Don't spend too much time on this, as it will most probably change. I suggest you spend about 3 minutes on it.

2. Then take the values that are at position 1 (value 1, i.e. Honesty) and position 2 (value 2, i.e. Creativity). Look at them and ask yourself the question: 'I can have Honesty but I can't have Creativity', then 'I can have Creativity but I can't have Honesty. You basically force yourself to choose between the two values. See which sounds right to you. If you can't be without value 2 (Creativity) and it sounds right, move it up a position. It is very important to ask yourself both ways and out loud to see which one sounds better as your brain will then make the decision easier for you.

3. You then take the value that is now at position 2 (i.e. Honesty) and the value that is at position 3 (i.e. Fun) and ask yourself the same question again, in both ways. If value 3 (i.e. Fun) moves up, you will then have to compare it to value 1 (i.e. Creativity) to see if it moves up even further.

4. You always decide between the two values that are next to each other. And if a position changes, you compare the values that are then next to each other.

5. Once you have done that, you will have your final order of values.

Examples of values

It is important that you **brainstorm your own values first** before you 'get inspired' by other value lists. Otherwise, you will limit your mind to the ones that are in front of you and you might forget a very important value.

And here are a few more examples of values:

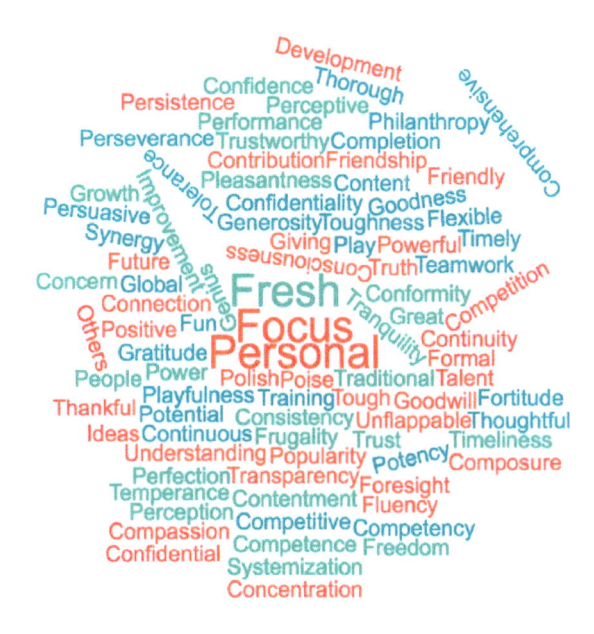

Development
Confidence Thorough
Persistence Perceptive
Performance Philanthropy
Perseverance Trustworthy Completion
Contribution Friendship
Pleasantness Content Friendly
Growth Confidentiality Goodness
Persuasive Generosity Toughness Flexible
Synergy Giving Play Powerful Timely
Future Conscious Truth Teamwork
Concern Global Fresh Conformity
Connection Great
Positive Fun Focus Continuity
Gratitude Personal Formal
People Power Polish Poise Traditional Talent
Playfulness Training Tough Goodwill Fortitude
Thankful Potential Consistency Unflappable Thoughtful
Ideas Continuous Frugality Trust Timeliness
Understanding Popularity Potency Composure
Perfection Transparency Foresight
Temperance Contentment Fluency
Perception Competitive Competency
Compassion Competence Freedom
Confidential Systemization
Concentration

73

Respect
Different
Resilience
Industry
Recognition
International
Relationships
Inquisitive
Dignity
Accessibility
Insightful
Inspiration
Devout
Accurate
Justice
Eagerness
Affection
Restraint
Anti-Corporate
Accuracy
Resolution
Drive
Resourcefulness
Aggressiveness
Diligence
Anti-Bureaucratic
Intuitive
Responsibility
Discretion
Informal
Innovative
Intensity
Duty
Use
Irreverence
Invention
Reflection
Recreation
Activity
Knowledge
Dreaming
Dominance
Investing
Resolve
Aggressive
Alertness
Investment
Rigor
Reliability
Reverence
Education
Kindness
Anticipation
Refined
Ease
Diversity
Alert
Individual
Resourceful
Reason
Depth
Down-to-Earth
Inviting
Anticipate
Direct
Determined
Economy
Altruism
Others
Intuition
Intelligence
Irreverent
Agility
Leadership
Discipline
Reliable
Resolute
Ambition
Discovery
Joy
Insight
Affective
Rest
Responsiveness
Innovation
Integrity
Dependability
Results
Results-Oriented
Devotion
Adaptability
Accountability
Amusement
Individuality
Adventure
Acceptance
Development
Adventurous
Relaxation
Accomplishment
Beyond
Directness
Determination

Customer
Value
Work
Quality
Creation
Credibility
Helpful
Uniqueness
Creative
Harmony
Unity
Pragmatic
Welcoming
Health
Worldwide
Impact
Holiness
Pursue
Prosperity
Balance
Utility
Vigor
Greatness
Impious
Cordiality
Curiosity
Humble
Decisive
Honor
Wealth
Daring
Prudence
Pursuit
Victory
Hygiene
Humor
Humility
Profits
Universal
Imagination
Vision
Democratic
Purity
Watchful
Realistic
Control
Virtue
Preservation
Warmth
Punctuality
Useful
Heart
History
Correct
Decency
Valor
Hope
Pride
Rational
Wonder
Service
Hopeful
Profitability
Professionalism
Practical
Hard
Impartial
Focus
Vital
Winning
Variety
Vitality
Watchfulness
Real
Courage
Proactive
Delight
Privacy
Customers
Wisdom
Growth
Work/Life
Progress
Hospitality
Unique
Heroism
Profane
Dedication
Satisfaction
Willfulness
Prepared
Improvement
Happiness
Precision
Craftiness
Independence
Precise
Proactively
Conviction
Decisiveness
Courtesy
Guidance
Creativity
Coordination
Cunning
Honesty
Cooperation
Productivity
Victorious
Craftsmanship

75

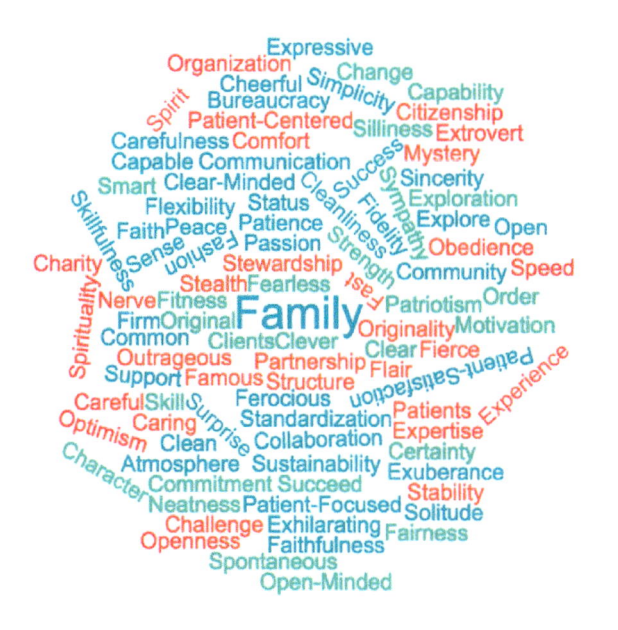

List your top 10 values here:

Knowing is not enough

The quote "**Knowing something is half the battle**" is a popular phrase from the GI Joe cartoon and comic book series. While it may be true that gaining knowledge or information is an important step towards achieving a goal, it is **not necessarily true that simply knowing something is enough** to put it into practice.

In order to truly put knowledge or information into practice, we often need to engage in intentional action and behavior change. For example, simply knowing that exercise is important for physical health does not necessarily mean that we will automatically begin exercising regularly. It requires effort, motivation, and the development of new habits and routines.

Furthermore, there may be external or internal barriers that prevent us from putting knowledge into practice, such as lack of resources, competing priorities, or self-doubt. In these cases, additional support or resources may be necessary to help us overcome these barriers and take action towards our goals.

In summary, while gaining knowledge or information is an important step towards achieving a goal, it is not necessarily sufficient on its own. To put knowledge into practice, we often need to engage in intentional action and behavior change, and may require additional support or resources to overcome external or internal barriers.

What specific knowledge or skills do I need to put into practice?

What external barriers or obstacles might prevent me from putting my knowledge into practice?

What internal barriers or obstacles might prevent me from taking action and changing my behavior?

How can I overcome these external and internal barriers?

What support or resources do I need to help me put my knowledge into practice?

What steps can I take to make sure I am accountable and stay on track with my behavior change goals?

How can I measure my progress towards putting my knowledge into practice?

What are some potential risks or challenges that may arise during the process of putting my knowledge into practice?

How can I adjust my approach if I encounter challenges or setbacks?

What are some potential benefits or rewards that I might experience once I successfully put my knowledge into practice?

Make Sure You're Ready

Make sure you are ready

Let's look at the **M in SMILE** - Make sure you are ready.

Cultivating a happy mindset involves several practices that can help improve one's overall well-being. One of the most effective ways to cultivate a happy mindset is to practice **gratitude** regularly. This involves focusing on the good things in one's life and expressing gratitude for them, whether it's through journaling, meditation, or simply expressing appreciation to others. Another practice is **mindfulness**, which involves being present in the moment and observing one's thoughts and emotions without judgment. Regular exercise and **physical activity** can also improve one's mood and promote a positive mindset. Developing strong **social connections** and engaging in **acts of kindness** and service can also promote happiness and well-being. Additionally, focusing on personal growth and learning can provide a sense of purpose and fulfillment. Overall, cultivating a happy mindset involves a combination of these practices, along with **patience and persistence**.

Here are some suggestions for things that can help you be ready for happiness in your life.

Cultivate a positive mindset

Your mindset can greatly affect how you perceive the world and your experiences in it. Try to **focus on the positive aspects of your life**, practice **gratitude**, and **reframe negative thoughts**.

Our thoughts can be our best friend or our worst enemy. They have the power to shape our perceptions of the world, influence our emotions, and impact our behaviors.

When our thoughts are **positive and supportive, they can help us to feel confident, motivated, and inspired.** They can encourage us to take positive actions and overcome obstacles. Positive thoughts can also help us to cultivate gratitude, optimism, and joy in our lives.

However, when our thoughts are **negative and self-critical**, they can become our **worst enemy**. Negative thoughts can lead to feelings of anxiety, depression, and low self-esteem. They can also cause us to act in ways that are harmful to ourselves and others.

The good news is that **we have the power to change our thoughts** and cultivate a more positive mindset. We can practice mindfulness and become aware of our thoughts, learning to recognize when they are negative or unhelpful. We can then challenge these thoughts and replace them with more positive and supportive ones.

What are the benefits of cultivating a positive mindset?

How can I develop a positive mindset when facing challenging situations?

What are some common negative thought patterns, and how can I reframe them in a positive way?

How can practicing gratitude help cultivate a positive mindset?

What role does self-talk play in developing a positive mindset, and how can I improve your self-talk?

How can mindfulness practices such as meditation and breathing exercises help cultivate a positive mindset?

How can physical exercise and healthy habits contribute to a positive mindset?

What are some practical strategies for maintaining a positive mindset over the long term?

How can surrounding yourself with positive people and engaging in positive activities support a positive mindset?

What are some common challenges people face when trying to develop a positive mindset, and how can they be overcome?

Take care of your physical health

Your physical health can have a big impact on your overall well-being. Make sure to **eat a healthy diet**, **exercise** regularly, and get enough **sleep**.

Am I getting enough sleep to feel rested and energized throughout the day?

How can I make small changes to my diet to eat healthier and support my physical health?

What physical activities do I enjoy that I can incorporate into my daily routine to exercise regularly?

Do I have any bad habits that are impacting my physical health, and how can I work to change them?

How can I stay motivated to take care of my physical health, even when I'm feeling tired or stressed?

Am I making time for self-care activities that support my physical health, such as taking relaxing baths or getting massages?

How can I find a balance between work and physical activity to ensure that I'm not neglecting one for the other?

What resources are available to help me learn more about nutrition and exercise, and how can I use them to improve my physical health?

What physical health goals do I want to achieve, and what steps can I take to work towards them?

How can I celebrate and appreciate my progress in taking care of my physical health, even when I face setbacks or challenges?

Foster strong relationships

Strong social connections are an important factor in happiness. Make time for your loved ones and **build meaningful relationships.**

Am I making time for my loved ones and nurturing my relationships with them?

How can I improve my communication skills to better connect with the people in my life?

Are there any past relationships that I need to repair, and how can I go about doing so?

Am I making an effort to meet new people and expand my social network?

How can I be a better listener and support system for the people in my life?

What values do I want my relationships to reflect, and how can I work to embody those values?

How can I balance my social life with other commitments and responsibilities, such as work or family?

Are there any toxic relationships in my life that I need to let go of in order to build stronger, more positive connections?

What activities or hobbies can I do with my loved ones to strengthen our bonds and create happy memories together?

How can I express gratitude for the people in my life and show them how much they mean to me?

Pursue meaningful goals

Having goals and working towards them can give you a **sense of purpose and fulfillment**. Identify what you truly value and set goals that **align with those values**.

Am I clear on what I truly value in life, and how can I align my goals with those values?

What steps can I take to break down my larger goals into smaller, achievable milestones?

How can I hold myself accountable to my goals and stay motivated, even when facing setbacks or challenges?

Are my goals realistic and attainable, or do I need to adjust them to make them more achievable?

How can I celebrate my progress towards my goals, even when I haven't yet reached the end result?

Are there any limiting beliefs or fears that are holding me back from pursuing my goals, and how can I work to overcome them?

How can I find a balance between pursuing my goals and taking care of myself and my relationships with others?

Are there any goals that I need to let go of in order to focus on those that truly align with my values?

How can I find support and guidance as I work towards my goals, such as through a mentor or accountability partner?

How can I adjust my goals as I grow and change, in order to ensure that they continue to align with my values and bring me fulfillment?

Practice self-care

Take time to do things that bring you **joy and relaxation**, whether it's taking a bubble bath, reading a book, or going for a walk in nature.

Am I making time for self-care activities on a regular basis, and how can I prioritize these activities in my life?

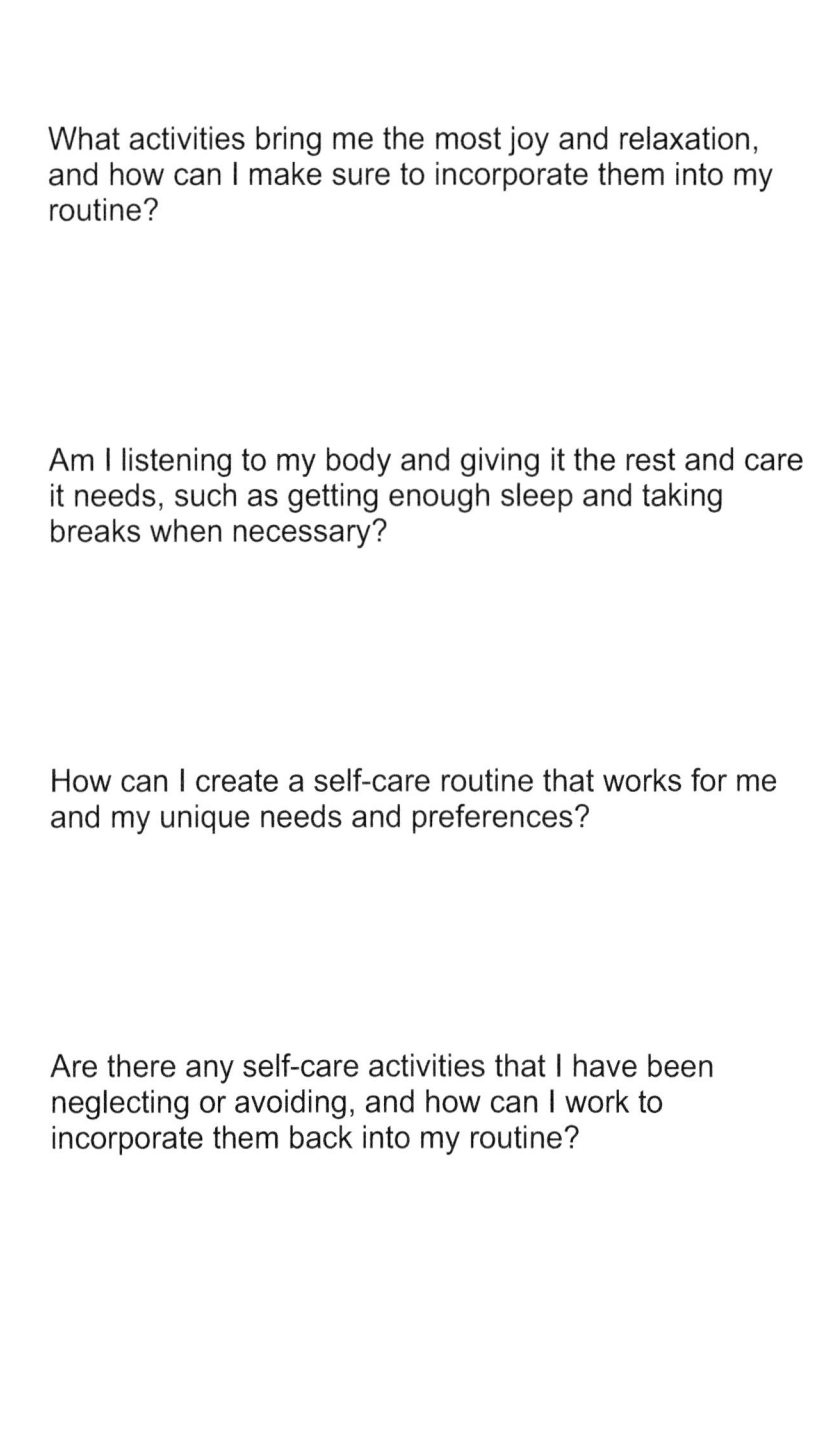

What activities bring me the most joy and relaxation, and how can I make sure to incorporate them into my routine?

Am I listening to my body and giving it the rest and care it needs, such as getting enough sleep and taking breaks when necessary?

How can I create a self-care routine that works for me and my unique needs and preferences?

Are there any self-care activities that I have been neglecting or avoiding, and how can I work to incorporate them back into my routine?

How can I find a balance between self-care and other responsibilities in my life, such as work or family?

What resources are available to help me learn more about self-care and how to make it a regular part of my routine?

How can I use mindfulness and meditation practices to enhance my self-care routine?

What self-care activities can I do with others, such as friends or family, to enhance my social connections while also taking care of myself?

How can I make self-care a priority, even when facing stress or challenging situations?

Be open to new experiences

Trying new things can be scary, but it can also lead to growth and happiness. **Embrace new experiences and challenges**, and be open to learning and growing.

Am I open to trying new things, even if they are outside of my comfort zone?

How can I challenge myself to step outside of my routine and try something new and different?

Are there any limiting beliefs or fears that are holding me back from trying new things, and how can I work to overcome them?

How can I stay open-minded and curious about new experiences, even if they don't immediately seem like something I would enjoy?

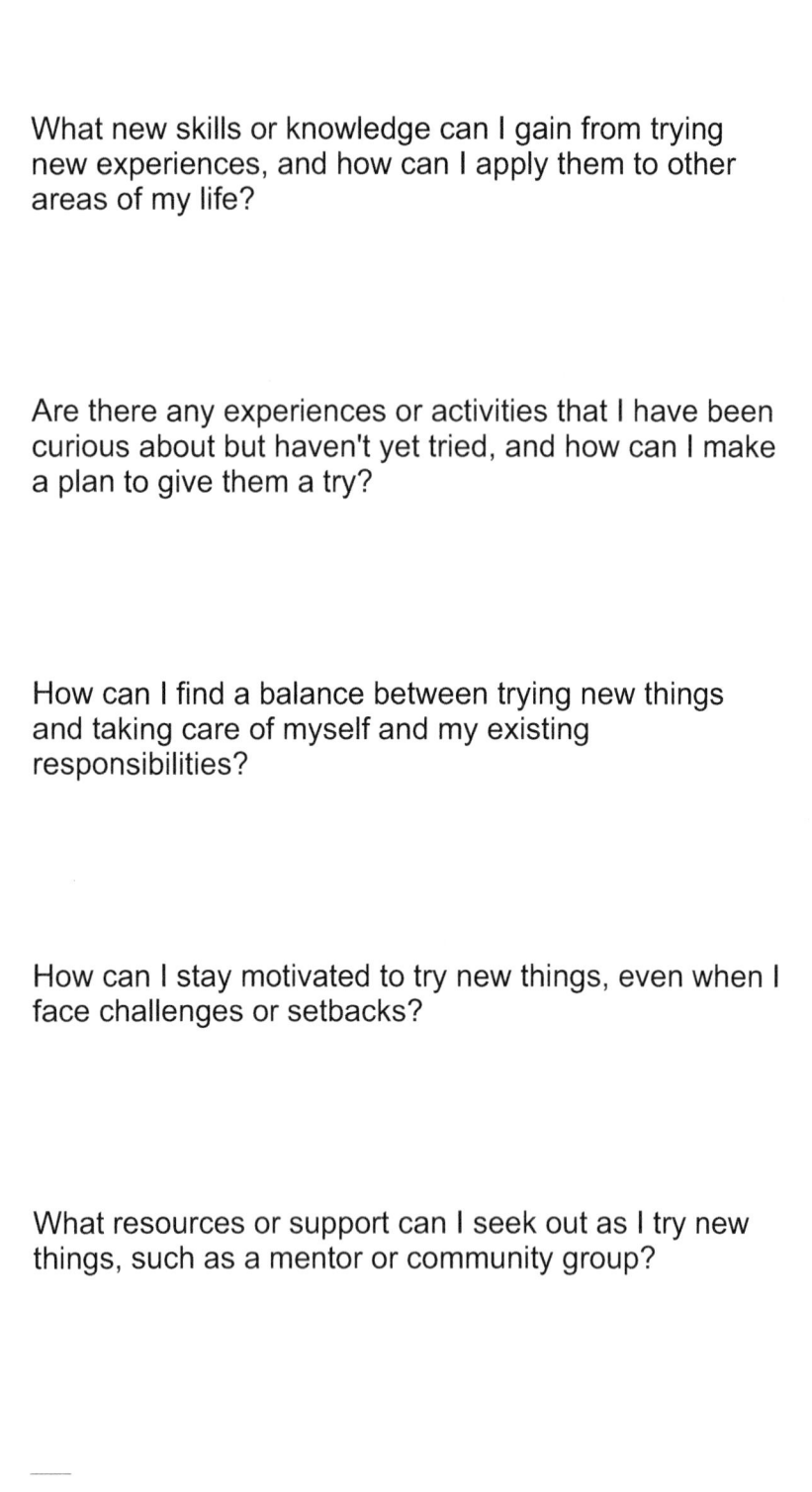

What new skills or knowledge can I gain from trying new experiences, and how can I apply them to other areas of my life?

Are there any experiences or activities that I have been curious about but haven't yet tried, and how can I make a plan to give them a try?

How can I find a balance between trying new things and taking care of myself and my existing responsibilities?

How can I stay motivated to try new things, even when I face challenges or setbacks?

What resources or support can I seek out as I try new things, such as a mentor or community group?

How can I celebrate my successes and lessons learned from trying new things, even if the experience didn't turn out exactly as I expected?

Remember that happiness is a journey, not a destination. It's important to be patient and kind to yourself as you work towards greater happiness in your life.

Self-awareness

Self-awareness is a crucial element in cultivating happiness. It involves **understanding your emotions, thoughts, and actions**, and how they contribute to your overall well-being. By being self-aware, you can identify the triggers that lead to negative emotions and thoughts, and work towards managing them more effectively. Self-awareness **also enables you to recognize your strengths and weaknesses**, which can guide you towards setting realistic goals and expectations for yourself. Through self-reflection and introspection, you can gain a **deeper understanding of yourself** and your values, allowing you to live a more authentic and fulfilling life. Ultimately, self-awareness is a key component in achieving happiness, as it helps you to be more mindful, intentional, and in control of your thoughts and emotions.

What are my strengths and weaknesses?

How do I react to stress or difficult situations?

What are my core values and beliefs?

How do I treat others, and how do I want to be treated?

What are my personal goals and aspirations?

How do I spend my time, and is it aligned with my values and goals?

How do I take care of my physical and mental health?

How do I cope with negative emotions, such as anger or sadness?

What brings me joy and fulfillment in life?

How can I improve my relationships with others and deepen my connections?

NLP techniques

NLP, or neuro-linguistic programming, offers a range of techniques that can help us to cultivate the right mindset for happiness. Here are a few examples:

Reframing

Reframing is a technique that **involves changing the way we think about a situation**. By reframing negative thoughts and beliefs into positive ones, we can change our perspective and create a more positive outlook on life. For example, instead of thinking "I'm not good enough," we can reframe it to "I am capable of achieving my goals."

Here are some steps you can take to practice reframing:

Identify negative thoughts and beliefs

Start by **noticing** when **negative thoughts** or beliefs come up in your mind. These may be thoughts like "I'm not good enough," "I'll never be able to do this," or "Things always go wrong for me." **Make a note** of these thoughts, as they will be the focus of your reframing practice.

Challenge negative thoughts

Once you've identified negative thoughts and beliefs, it's time to challenge them. **Ask yourself if these thoughts are really true** or if they're just limiting beliefs that are holding you back. Consider if there is any evidence to support these negative thoughts, or if they are simply assumptions that you have made.

Reframe negative thoughts

After challenging negative thoughts, it's time to **reframe them into positive ones.** Start by identifying the opposite of the negative thought. For example, if your negative thought is "I'm not good enough," the opposite could be "I am capable and deserving of success." Next, create a statement that reflects the positive reframed thought. This statement should be in the present tense, use positive language, and feel true and empowering to you.

Practice reframing regularly

Reframing is a skill that takes practice. **Set aside time each day to practice reframing** negative thoughts into positive ones. You can do this by journaling, repeating affirmations, or simply taking a few minutes to reflect on your thoughts and feelings.

You can find a downloadable journal on this page:
www.creativestartupacademy.com/resources-hf

Use reframing in real-life situations

Reframing can be particularly helpful in challenging or difficult situations. **When faced with a problem or setback, try to reframe the situation in a positive light.** For example, if you receive negative feedback at work, instead of thinking "I'm a failure," reframe it to "I can learn from this feedback and improve my performance."

By practicing reframing regularly, you can shift your perspective and create a more positive outlook on life. Remember that it takes time and effort to change your thoughts and beliefs, but with practice, you can cultivate a more positive mindset and achieve greater happiness and fulfillment.

Anchoring

Anchoring is a technique that involves **associating a particular feeling or state of mind with a specific trigger or anchor.** By creating an anchor for positive emotions such as joy, love, and gratitude, we can bring them up at will and feel them more intensely. For example, we can create an anchor by recalling a happy memory and associating it with a physical gesture such as pressing our thumb and index finger together.

Here's how you can practice anchoring:

Choose a positive emotion

The first step in anchoring is to **choose a positive emotion** that you want to anchor. This could be anything from joy and love to gratitude and confidence.

Recall a powerful experience

Once you've chosen a positive emotion, **recall a powerful experience** in which you felt that emotion. This could be a specific memory, an image, or a feeling. Try to make the experience as vivid and detailed as possible, and allow yourself to **fully immerse** in the positive emotion.

Choose an anchor

Next, choose a **physical anchor** that you can associate with the positive emotion. This could be a gesture such as pressing your thumb and index finger together, or a touch such as tapping your chest.

Create the anchor: To create the anchor, associate the physical gesture or touch with the positive emotion by repeating the gesture or touch several times while fully immersing yourself in the positive emotion.

Practice the anchor

Once you've created the anchor, **practice it regularly**. Every time you want to access the positive emotion, repeat the physical gesture or touch to activate the anchor. Over time, the anchor will become stronger and you will be able to access the positive emotion more easily and consistently.

Use the anchor in real-life situations

Anchoring can be **particularly helpful in challenging or stressful situations**. When faced with a difficult situation, use the anchor to access the positive emotion and approach the situation with a more positive and empowered mindset.

By practicing anchoring regularly, you can train your mind to access positive emotions **more easily and consistently**, which can lead to greater happiness and fulfillment in your life. Remember that it takes time and effort to create and strengthen an anchor, but with practice, you can develop a powerful tool for cultivating positivity and resilience.

Visualization

Visualization is a technique that involves **creating mental images of desired outcomes or experiences.** By visualizing ourselves achieving our goals and experiencing positive emotions, we can create a sense of motivation and positivity. Visualization can also help us to overcome limiting beliefs and visualize new possibilities for ourselves.

Here's how you can practice visualization in a practical way:

Choose a goal or desired outcome

The first step in visualization is **to choose a goal or desired outcome** that you want to achieve. This could be anything from landing a new job to improving your health or achieving a personal goal.

Create a clear mental image

Once you've chosen your goal, create a clear mental image of yourself achieving that goal. Try to make the image as **vivid and detailed** as possible, using all your senses to create a full sensory experience.

Focus on positive emotions

As you visualize yourself achieving your goal, **focus on the positive emotions associated with it**, such as joy, gratitude, and satisfaction. Allow yourself to fully immerse in these emotions and feel them as if they are happening in the present moment.

Practice regularly

To make visualization effective, it's important to practice it regularly. **Set aside a few minutes each day** to visualize yourself achieving your goal and experiencing the associated positive emotions.

Use affirmations

Affirmations are **positive statements** that reinforce the beliefs and outcomes you want to achieve. Use affirmations to **support your visualization practice**, such as "I am capable of achieving my goals" or "I am worthy of success and happiness."

Here are some affirmations that you can use:
- I choose to focus on the positive aspects of my life.
- I am worthy of love and happiness.
- Every day is a new opportunity to create joy and positivity in my life.
- I am grateful for all the blessings in my life, big and small.
- I trust that everything will work out for my highest good.
- I am surrounded by abundance and positivity.
- I am capable of achieving my goals and dreams.
- I am filled with inner peace and contentment.
- I release all negative thoughts and emotions and embrace happiness.
- I choose to live in the present moment and appreciate the beauty around me.

Take action

Visualization is a powerful tool for motivating and inspiring you to take action towards your goals. Use the positive energy and motivation generated by your visualization practice **to take tangible steps towards achieving your desired outcome.**

By practicing visualization regularly and incorporating it into your daily routine, you can create a powerful tool for **cultivating positivity, motivation, and resilience** in your life. Remember that visualization is most effective when combined with action, so be sure to take concrete steps towards achieving your goals as well.

Here are some questions that help you with it:

What specific actions can I take today to move closer to my goal?

What resources or skills do I need to acquire to achieve my goal?

What potential obstacles or challenges might I face, and how can I overcome them?

What is my timeline for achieving this goal, and what benchmarks can I set to track my progress?

Who can I reach out to for support or guidance in pursuing my goal?

How will achieving this goal positively impact my life and the lives of those around me?

What sacrifices or trade-offs am I willing to make to achieve this goal?

How can I break down this goal into smaller, more manageable tasks?

What daily habits or routines can I establish to keep me focused and motivated?

How will I celebrate and reward myself for achieving this goal?

Practice self-compassion

Practice self-compassion by **being kind and gentle with yourself.** Treat yourself as you would treat a good friend, offering words of encouragement and support. Acknowledge that it's okay to make mistakes and that you are not alone in your struggles.

Answer the following questions:

What do I need right now to feel cared for and supported?

How can I offer myself kindness and understanding at this moment?

What are some ways I can speak to myself with greater compassion and self-love?

How can I reframe my self-critical thoughts in a more positive and constructive way?

What would I say to a friend who is going through the same struggle or difficulty that I am currently facing?

What are some things that I appreciate and value about myself?

How can I prioritize my own needs and self-care without feeling guilty or selfish?

What are some things I can do to nurture my physical, emotional, and mental well-being?

How can I approach my mistakes and failures with greater self-compassion and understanding?

What are some ways I can celebrate and acknowledge my own strengths, accomplishments, and progress?

Focus on strengths and accomplishments

Focus on your **strengths** and **accomplishments** rather than your weaknesses and failures. **Celebrate** your successes, no matter how small, and use them as motivation to continue moving forward.

Here are some questions that help you focus on your strengths.

What are some skills or talents that come easily to me?

What are some positive feedback or compliments that I have received from others in the past?

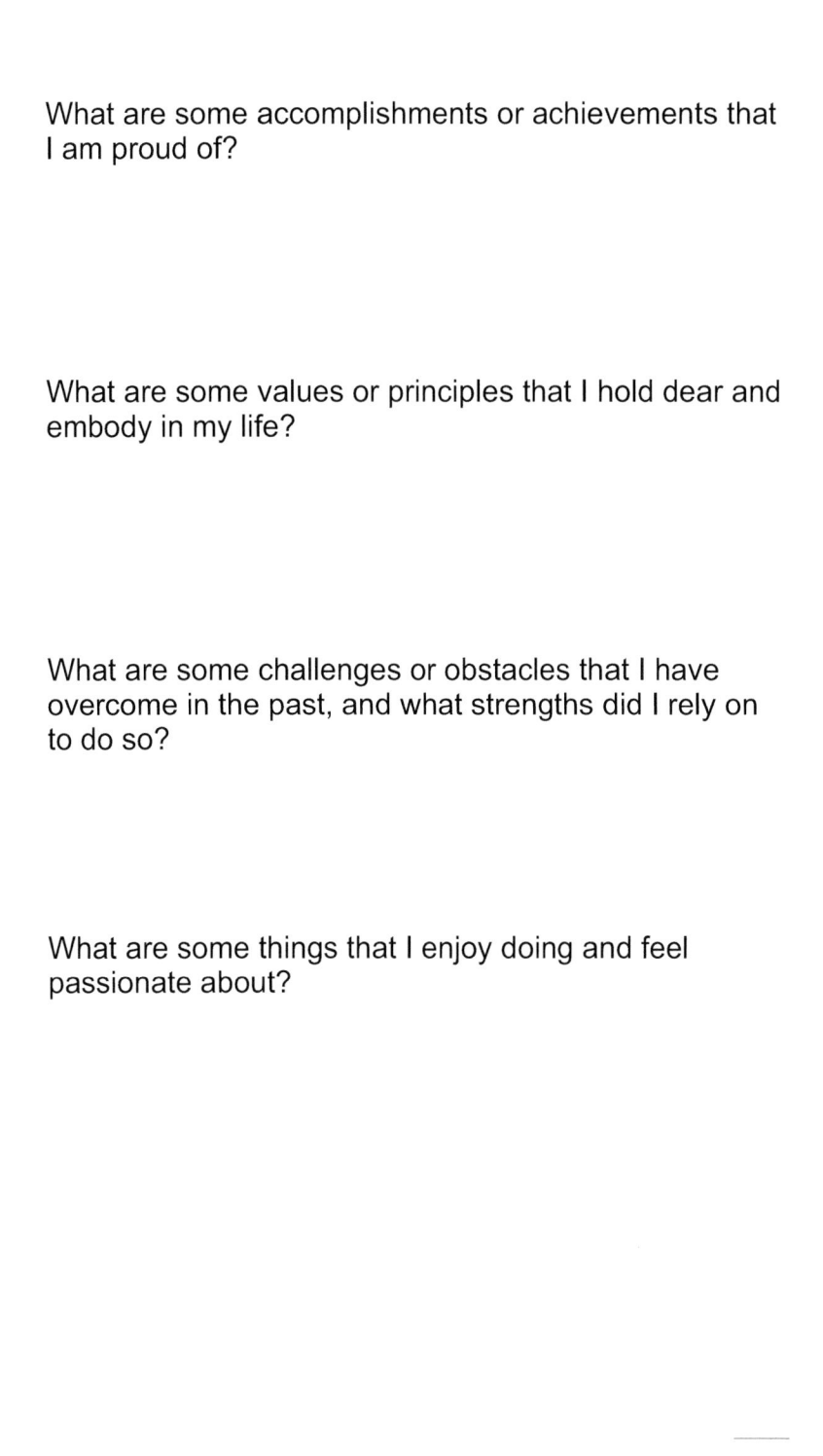

What are some accomplishments or achievements that I am proud of?

What are some values or principles that I hold dear and embody in my life?

What are some challenges or obstacles that I have overcome in the past, and what strengths did I rely on to do so?

What are some things that I enjoy doing and feel passionate about?

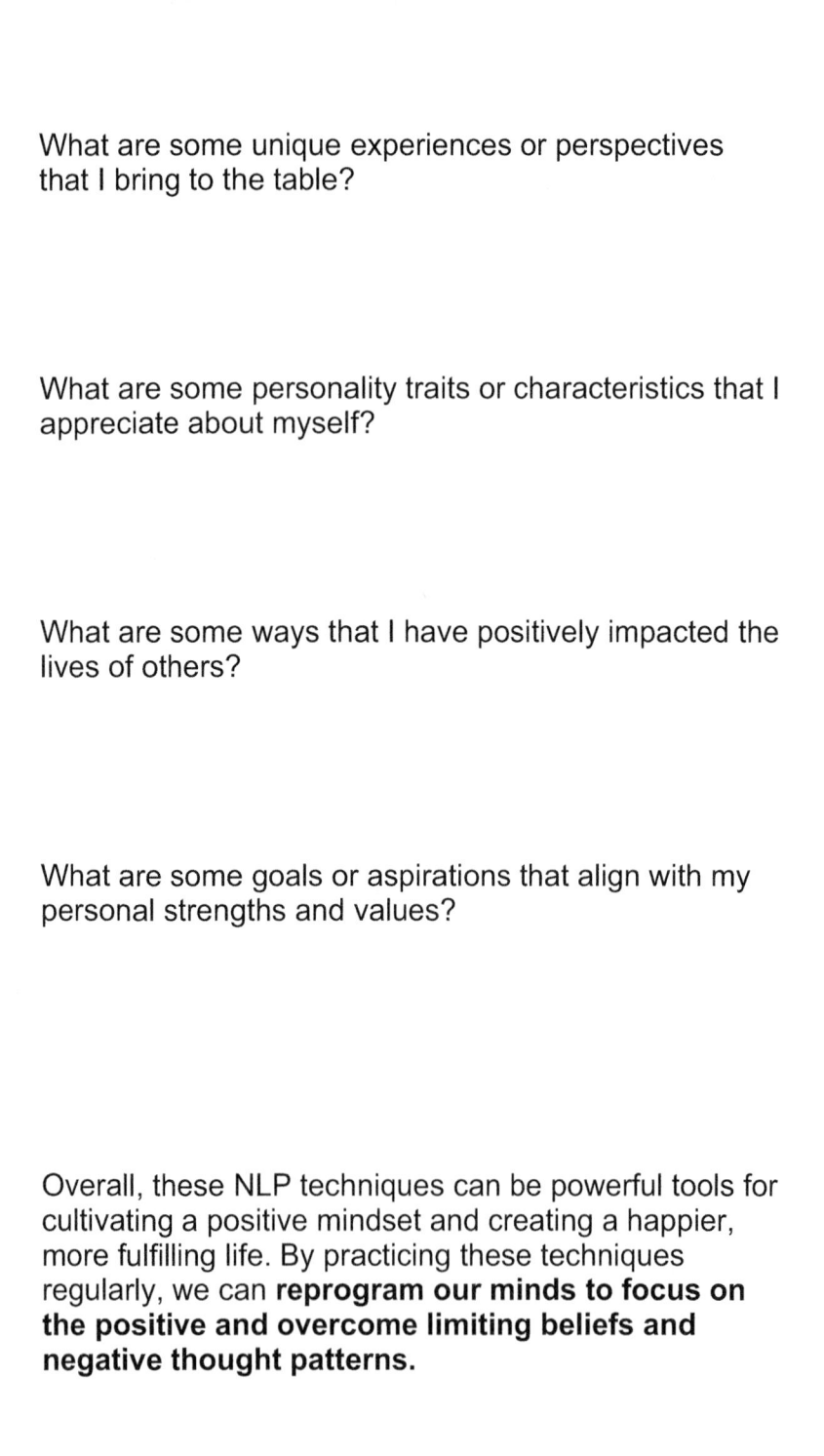

What are some unique experiences or perspectives that I bring to the table?

What are some personality traits or characteristics that I appreciate about myself?

What are some ways that I have positively impacted the lives of others?

What are some goals or aspirations that align with my personal strengths and values?

Overall, these NLP techniques can be powerful tools for cultivating a positive mindset and creating a happier, more fulfilling life. By practicing these techniques regularly, we can **reprogram our minds to focus on the positive and overcome limiting beliefs and negative thought patterns.**

Implant Happiness into Your Brain

Implant happiness into your brain

Let's now look at the **I in SMILE** - Implant happiness into your brain.

Let's now delve into **the factors that contribute to happiness and those that do not**, based on findings from **research**. Before we dive into exploring ways to enhance our happiness, let's first take a closer look at what's happening in our brains and discover how we can use specific techniques to create positive changes.

Neuroplasticity

Neuroplasticity refers to the brain's ability to **change and reorganize itself throughout a person's life**. This means that the structure and function of the brain **can be altered** by experiences, learning, and other environmental factors. One powerful way to harness the power of neuroplasticity is through **mindfulness meditation**.

Mindfulness meditation **involves focusing your attention on the present moment** and becoming aware of your thoughts, feelings, and bodily sensations without judgment. This practice has been shown to have many benefits for mental and physical health, including **reducing stress and anxiety**, **improving sleep**, and **boosting immune function**.

Research has also shown that mindfulness meditation can lead to **changes in the brain's structure and function**. Studies have found that regular meditation practice can **increase the thickness of the prefrontal**

cortex, a part of the brain associated with attention, decision-making, and self-awareness. Meditation has also been found to **increase** the **size** of the **hippocampus**, a brain region involved in memory and learning.

In addition, mindfulness meditation has been shown to **reduce activity in the amygdala**, a part of the brain associated with fear and stress. This can lead to a reduction in the "fight or flight" response and **a greater sense of calm** and well-being.

Overall, mindfulness meditation is a powerful tool for **promoting neuroplasticity** and changing the brain in positive ways. By incorporating mindfulness practice into your daily routine, you can cultivate greater emotional regulation, cognitive flexibility, and resilience, all of which are important for achieving happiness and well-being.

Go through these questions to become more mindful:

What physical sensations do I feel in my body right now, and can I observe them without reacting or judging them?

What emotions am I experiencing in this moment, and can I simply acknowledge them without getting lost in the stories or judgments that surround them?

What thoughts are coming up in my mind, and can I observe them as if they were clouds passing by in the sky, without getting attached to them or trying to push them away?

How can I use mindfulness to become more aware of my automatic, habitual reactions to different situations, and begin to respond with greater intention and awareness instead?

What are some specific mindfulness practices I can incorporate into my daily routine, such as mindful breathing, body scanning, or mindful eating, to cultivate greater awareness and presence in my life?

How can I use mindfulness to cultivate a greater sense of compassion and empathy towards myself and others, and to develop more meaningful relationships?

What obstacles or challenges might I encounter as I begin to practice mindfulness, and how can I approach them with curiosity, openness, and non-judgment?

How can I use mindfulness to develop greater self-awareness and insight into my own patterns of behavior, thought, and emotion, and to cultivate a greater sense of purpose and direction in my life?

How can I use mindfulness to cultivate greater resilience, emotional balance, and overall well-being in the face of stress, adversity, or challenging life circumstances?

How can I use mindfulness to connect more deeply with the world around me, and to cultivate a greater sense of gratitude, awe, and wonder for the beauty and complexity of life?

Amygdala

The amygdala is a small, almond-shaped structure located deep within the temporal lobe of the brain. It plays a **key role in processing emotions**, particularly fear and anxiety. When we experience stress, the amygdala becomes more active, releasing a flood of stress hormones throughout the body that can trigger the fight-or-flight response.

Research has shown that **chronic stress can cause the amygdala to become hyperactive**, leading to increased anxiety and difficulty regulating emotions. In addition, prolonged activation of the amygdala can actually cause physical changes in the brain, leading to a reduction in the size and connectivity of certain brain regions involved in emotion regulation.

Mindfulness meditation has been shown to be an effective way to **reduce amygdala activity** and improve emotion regulation. By training the mind to focus on the present moment without judgment, mindfulness can help individuals become more aware of their emotions and learn to respond to stress in a more balanced and adaptive way.

Studies have shown that regular mindfulness meditation can actually cause **physical changes in the brain,** increasing the size and connectivity of certain regions involved in emotion regulation while decreasing activity in the amygdala. This suggests that mindfulness meditation may be a powerful tool for promoting emotional well-being and resilience, and may even help to protect against the negative effects of chronic stress on the brain.

The **amygdala is actually known to decrease in density**, or gray matter volume, following a **reduction in stress.** This is because chronic stress can cause structural changes in the brain, including atrophy in the amygdala and prefrontal cortex, which can result in a reduced ability to regulate emotions and respond to stressors effectively.

Mindfulness meditation has been found to be a particularly effective tool for **reducing stress and associated changes in the brain**. In fact, studies have shown that practicing mindfulness meditation can lead to an **increase in gray matter density in the prefrontal** cortex, which is involved in attention regulation and emotion regulation, as well as a **decrease in gray matter density in the amygdala**. This suggests that mindfulness meditation may help to restore balance to the brain and improve our ability to manage stress and regulate our emotions.

Additionally, mindfulness meditation has been found to **increase activity in the left prefrontal cortex**, which is associated with positive emotions, and to decrease activity in the amygdala during stressful situations, indicating a more measured response to stress. This can help individuals to maintain a more positive outlook, reduce anxiety and depression, and improve overall well-being.

Default network

The default network in the brain is **always active**, even when we're not focused on a specific task. The **default mode network (DMN)** includes regions such as the medial prefrontal cortex, posterior cingulate cortex, and inferior parietal lobule. These regions are known to be involved in self-referential thinking, mental simulation, and autobiographical memory, among other functions.

While the DMN can be **useful for things like planning and problem-solving**, it can also lead **to mind wandering** when we're not engaged in a task. The mind wandering state involves a shift of attention away from the present moment and into thoughts unrelated to the task at hand, often including ruminations about the past or worries about the future.

Research has shown that **mind wandering can have negative effects on our mood and well-being**, and is associated with increased levels of stress, anxiety, and depression. On the other hand, mindfulness practices and other techniques that help us **stay focused** on the present moment can have positive effects on our mental health and overall happiness.

Go through the following questions:

How much of my daily thinking is directed towards focused tasks, and how much is spent in more unstructured or free-form thinking?

Are there any particular activities or situations where I find myself more likely to engage in mind-wandering or daydreaming, and what might be some reasons for this?

How do my patterns of thinking and attention affect my overall well-being, productivity, and sense of purpose in life?

Are there any specific strategies or techniques that I use to manage my default network activity and stay more focused on tasks when needed, and how effective do I find them?

How can I strike a balance between allowing my mind to wander and engage in creative thinking, while also staying focused and productive when necessary?

How do external factors, such as stress, distractions, or technology, impact my default network activity and ability to stay focused on tasks?

How can I use mindfulness practices or other techniques to become more aware of my default network activity and learn to control it more effectively?

Are there any particular areas of my life, such as work or relationships, where my default network activity might be interfering with my ability to achieve my goals or meet my responsibilities?

How can I use my knowledge of the default network to better understand my own thinking patterns and tendencies, and work towards developing a more intentional and purposeful mindset?

How can I use my default network activity in a positive and productive way, such as by engaging in creative thinking or reflecting on my values and priorities?

What doesn't make us happy

Research has shown that thinking about **buying experiences can bring more happiness than thinking about a material purchase**. However, our brain often tends to convince us otherwise. The reason for this is that our brains have evolved to focus on tangible and material things that we can touch and feel, as these things have historically helped us survive and thrive as a species. **Material possessions that can eventually lose their novelty and meaning over time.**

Despite this knowledge, our brain often still tries to convince us that material possessions will bring us more happiness, as they offer a sense of security and status.

Social comparison

Social comparison is a **natural human tendency**, but it can have **negative effects on our happiness**. When we compare ourselves to others, especially on social media where people often showcase their best selves, we may start to feel inadequate, jealous, or unhappy with our own lives. Therefore, avoiding social comparison can be a helpful strategy for increasing happiness.

One way to avoid social comparison is to **limit or avoid social media altogether.** Social media can create an unrealistic and distorted view of other people's lives, which can be harmful to our self-esteem and happiness. If deleting social media accounts is not an option, it can be helpful to take **regular breaks** from social media or to follow accounts that promote positivity and inspire you to be your best self.

Another way to avoid social comparison is **to be conscious of the comparisons** we make and the reference points we use. We can choose to focus on our own journey and progress rather than comparing ourselves to others. **Practicing gratitude** can also help shift our focus from what we lack to what we have, and help us appreciate and enjoy the present moment.

Finally, when we notice ourselves engaging in social comparison, **we can use cognitive-behavioral techniques to break the pattern**. For example, we can shout out loud "stop" or replace negative thoughts with positive ones. By avoiding social comparison, we can increase our happiness and focus on our own unique journey in life.

Here are some questions you can answer for this topic:

How often do I compare myself to others, especially on social media?

What emotions do I typically experience when I engage in social comparison?

Am I being realistic in my social comparisons, or am I comparing myself to an unrealistic ideal?

How does social comparison affect my self-esteem and overall happiness?

What are some positive aspects of my life that I tend to overlook when I engage in social comparison?

How can I shift my focus from comparing myself to others to focusing on my own progress and accomplishments?

What are some strategies I can use to limit my exposure to social media and avoid engaging in social comparison?

How can I cultivate a sense of gratitude and contentment in my own life without comparing myself to others?

What are some healthy ways to challenge myself without comparing myself to others?

How can I use my experiences to help others who may be struggling with social comparison?

Affluence

Research has shown that the pursuit of wealth and material possessions doesn't necessarily lead to happiness. While **money** can provide a sense of security and basic needs, **it's not always the key to long-lasting happiness**. In fact, people who prioritize time over money tend to experience greater well-being and life satisfaction.

Valuing time over money means that individuals prioritize experiences, relationships, and personal growth over material possessions and career advancement. When people focus on time, they tend to engage in activities that are meaningful to them, such as spending time with loved ones, pursuing hobbies, and traveling.

Furthermore, when individuals prioritize time, they tend to **experience less stress, burnout, and work-life conflict.** They are more likely to have a work-life balance and feel a greater sense of control over their lives. In contrast, those who prioritize money often experience greater stress and work longer hours, which can lead to burnout and negative health outcomes.

In conclusion, **valuing time over money can lead to greater happiness and well-being**. It's important to **consider** our **priorities** and how we **allocate** our **time** and **resources**.

As usual, here are some questions for you to go through:

How important is wealth and material possessions in my life, and how much of it is driven by societal pressure or personal desire?

Have I ever experienced a sense of emptiness or lack of fulfillment, despite having wealth and material possessions?

What are some other factors in my life that contribute to my overall happiness and well-being, and how do they compare to the role of wealth and material possessions?

Have I ever felt envious or dissatisfied with others who have more wealth and material possessions than me, and how has this affected my happiness and sense of self-worth?

What are some ways in which I can cultivate happiness and satisfaction in my life that don't involve wealth and material possessions, such as relationships, hobbies, or personal growth?

How can I strike a balance between pursuing financial success and maintaining a healthy perspective on the role of wealth in my life?

How can I use my wealth and resources to make a positive impact on the world and contribute to the greater good, rather than solely focusing on my own personal gain?

How do cultural and societal values impact our beliefs and attitudes towards wealth and happiness, and how can we challenge these narratives to live a more fulfilling life?

How can I practice gratitude and appreciation for the things that truly matter in life, such as love, health, and personal growth, rather than constantly striving for more wealth and possessions?

What role do my personal values and beliefs play in my pursuit of happiness, and how can I align my actions and priorities with these values to live a more fulfilling life?

Status of fame

While there is a widespread belief that achieving high status or fame can lead to greater happiness and well-being, research suggests that this may not be the case. In fact, several studies have found that **individuals who are driven by a desire for status or fame tend to experience lower well-being and greater anxiety and depression.**

One reason for this is that the pursuit of status or fame can be inherently **stressful** and **competitive**, leading to feelings of **insecurity**, **jealousy**, and **social comparison**. In addition, the rewards of status and fame are often short-lived and superficial, leading to a sense of emptiness or dissatisfaction over time.

Furthermore, individuals who achieve high status or fame may face **unique challenges** that can impact their well-being. For example, they may experience increased scrutiny, criticism, or pressure to maintain their image or reputation, leading to feelings of anxiety, depression, or burnout.

Overall, while achieving a certain level of status or fame may provide **temporary benefits**, research suggests that it is not a reliable or sustainable path to long-term happiness or well-being. Instead, we should be focusing on meaningful relationships, personal growth, and a sense of purpose.

Beauty and attractiveness

While physical attractiveness can provide certain **short-term benefits**, such as increased **social attention** and **positive feedback**, research suggests that it may not have a significant impact on long-term happiness or well-being. In fact, several studies have found that **beauty or physical attractiveness may be associated with certain negative effects on well-being**.

One reason for this is that physical attractiveness is often associated with **external validation and social comparison**, leading individuals to focus on their appearance and seek validation from others rather than developing internal sources of happiness and fulfillment. This can lead to feelings of **insecurity**, **anxiety**, and **dissatisfaction** over time.

In addition, research suggests that physical attractiveness may be associated with certain **negative stereotypes** or assumptions, such as being seen as shallow or lacking substance. This can lead to feelings of social isolation or stigma, particularly if individuals rely heavily on their physical appearance for their sense of self-worth.

Furthermore, physical attractiveness is often subject to age-related changes, and individuals who rely heavily on their appearance may experience a **decline in their sense of self-worth** and well-being as they age.

Overall, while physical attractiveness can certainly provide certain short-term benefits, research suggests that it is not a reliable or sustainable source of long-term happiness or well-being.

Intelligence and academic achievement

While intelligence and academic achievement can certainly provide **certain benefits**, such as increased **career opportunities** and **intellectual stimulation**, research suggests that they may **not be reliable predictors of long-term happiness** or well-being.

One reason for this is that intelligence and academic achievement may be associated with certain negative **stereotypes** or **assumptions**, such as being seen as aloof or lacking social skills. This can lead to feelings of **social isolation or dissatisfaction**, particularly if individuals rely heavily on their intelligence or academic achievements for their sense of self-worth.

In addition, research suggests that high intelligence or academic achievement may be associated with certain **personality traits**, such as **perfectionism** or **anxiety**, which can lead to higher levels of stress and lower levels of happiness or well-being over time.

What makes us happy

So, what does make us happy? In this chapter, we will explore some of the **key findings** from recent research on happiness, and discover some practical strategies for cultivating greater happiness and well-being in our lives. From **healthy habit creation** to the power of gratitude, from savouring life's small moments to investing in meaningful experiences, we will delve into the various techniques and approaches that can help us lead happier, more fulfilling lives. Whether you are looking to **boost your mood**, overcome negative thought patterns, or simply cultivate a greater sense of inner peace and contentment, **the insights and tools** in this chapter are sure to provide valuable **guidance** and **inspiration**.

Healthy habits

Healthy habits are **behaviors that contribute to physical, mental, and emotional well-being**.

Developing healthy habits is essential for promoting overall well-being and happiness. These habits can help to **enhance physical health**, **mental health**, and **emotional resilience**, and can contribute to a greater sense of purpose and fulfillment in life. Healthy habits can include practices such as regular exercise, healthy eating, getting enough sleep, practicing mindfulness or meditation, spending time in nature, and engaging in hobbies or activities that bring joy.

For example, if you make it a habit to exercise regularly, you **may experience increased energy**,

improved mood, and **better physical health**. Similarly, if you make it a habit to practice gratitude every day, you may experience increased feelings of happiness and contentment.

The key to building positive habits is to **start small and be consistent**. It's easier to form a habit when you break it down into small, manageable steps. For example, if you want to start exercising regularly, start with just 10 minutes a day and gradually increase the time and intensity as you become more comfortable.

Another key to building healthy habits is **accountability**. Find a friend or family member who can support and encourage you in your journey, or join a group or class where you can connect with others who share similar goals. **Tracking your progress** and **celebrating your successes** can also help you stay motivated and committed to your healthy habits.

Finding situations that support us with implementing healthy habits such as sleep, social connection, and exercise is key to making them sustainable and beneficial for our happiness.

Consistency is also crucial when building habits. It's important to make the habit a regular part of your routine, so that it becomes automatic and second nature. This may mean setting aside specific times each day or week to engage in the habit, or finding ways to incorporate it into your existing routine.

It is often **easier** to build healthy habits if you **attach them to a daily task or routine**. When you associate a new habit with an existing routine or activity, it becomes more automatic and requires less effort to maintain. For example, if you want to start drinking more water throughout the day, you can associate this habit with an existing routine such as drinking a glass of water every time you finish a cup of coffee or tea.

Another benefit of attaching a new habit to a daily task is that it helps create a **sense of momentum and consistency.** When you perform a new habit every day at the same time or in the same context, it becomes part of your daily routine and feels more natural and achievable.

In terms of sleep, creating a **relaxing bedtime routine** and setting a consistent sleep schedule can help signal to our bodies that it's time for rest. Additionally, creating a comfortable sleep environment, such as a dark, quiet, and cool room, can help promote restful sleep.

Remember that building positive habits **takes time and effort, but the rewards can be significant**.

Here are some questions you can ask yourself with regards to creating healthy habits:

What are my current habits and routines? Which of these habits are healthy and which are not?

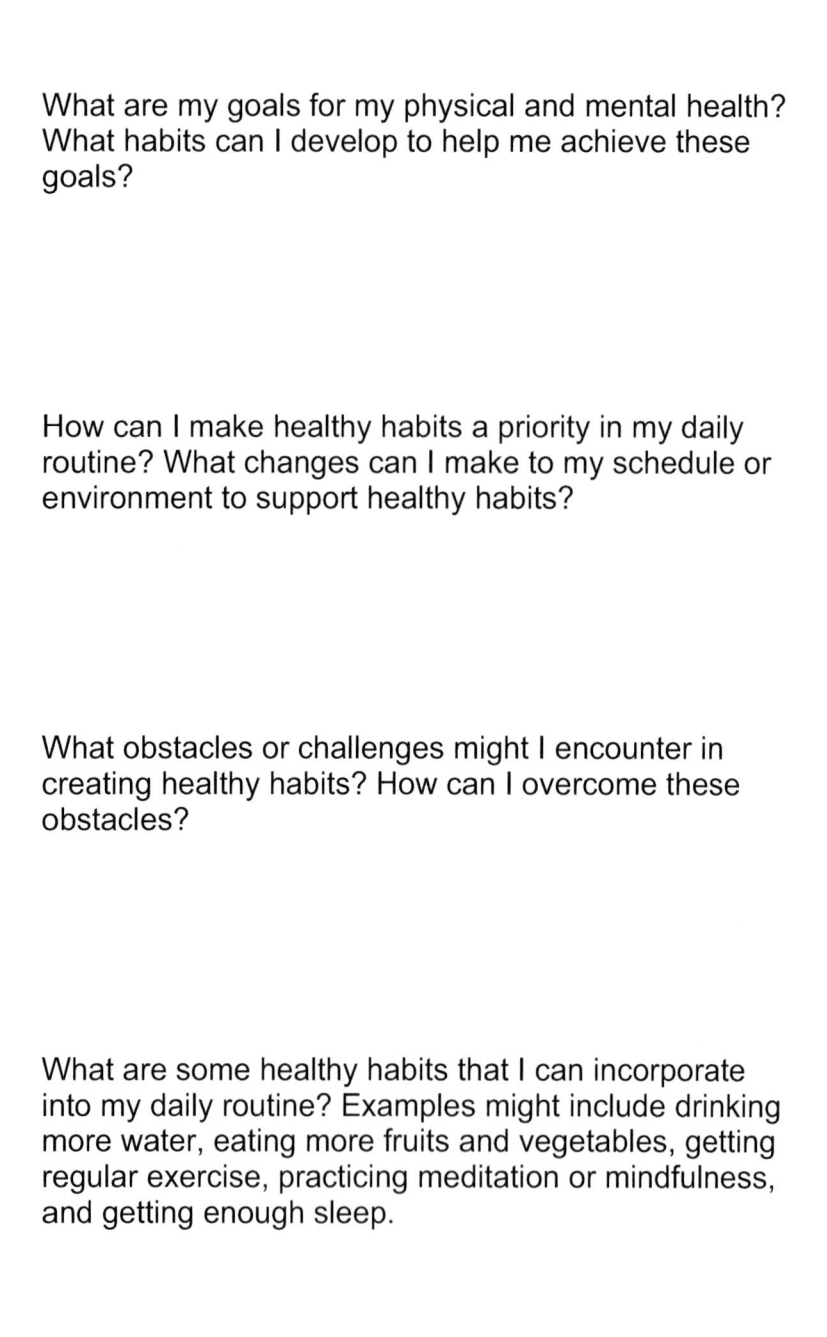

What are my goals for my physical and mental health? What habits can I develop to help me achieve these goals?

How can I make healthy habits a priority in my daily routine? What changes can I make to my schedule or environment to support healthy habits?

What obstacles or challenges might I encounter in creating healthy habits? How can I overcome these obstacles?

What are some healthy habits that I can incorporate into my daily routine? Examples might include drinking more water, eating more fruits and vegetables, getting regular exercise, practicing meditation or mindfulness, and getting enough sleep.

How can I track my progress in creating healthy habits? What tools or resources can I use to monitor my progress and stay accountable?

How can I make healthy habits enjoyable and sustainable in the long term? What can I do to make healthy habits a part of my lifestyle, rather than just a temporary change?

Investing into experiences

Investing in experiences, rather than material possessions, has been shown to be a powerful way to cultivate happiness. Experiences provide us **with lasting memories and a sense of personal growth**, which can contribute to a deeper sense of satisfaction and fulfillment than simply acquiring more stuff.

When we invest in experiences, we also tend to **prioritize our time and resources in a way that aligns with our values and personal interests**. This can lead to a greater sense of purpose and meaning in life, which are key drivers of overall well-being.

Some examples of experiences that can contribute to happiness include travel, trying new hobbies or activities, spending quality time with loved ones, and participating in meaningful community events or volunteer work. By **consciously choosing** to invest in these types of experiences, we can shift our focus away from the pursuit of material possessions and towards a more fulfilling and joyful life.

Furthermore, when we invest in experiences, we are not only **investing** in ourselves but also **in our relationships** with others. We can share our experiences with others and **create memories** that we can cherish and talk about for years to come. This means that we not only get to enjoy the experience ourselves, but we can also experience happiness from the social connections that come from sharing our experiences with others.

However, even though experiences tend to make us happier, our brains often try to convince us otherwise. We may be tempted to buy material possessions because our brains believe that they will bring us more happiness than experiences. This is because our brains have **a tendency to focus on the short-term pleasure** of acquiring something new rather than the long-term happiness that comes from experiences. Therefore, **it is important to be mindful** of this bias and actively choose to invest in experiences that will bring us more lasting happiness.

Here are some questions someone might ask themselves about investing into experiences:

What are some experiences that I've always wanted to have but haven't prioritized yet?

How do I believe investing in experiences differs from investing in material possessions?

What benefits do I expect to gain from investing in experiences, such as personal growth, new perspectives, or building relationships?

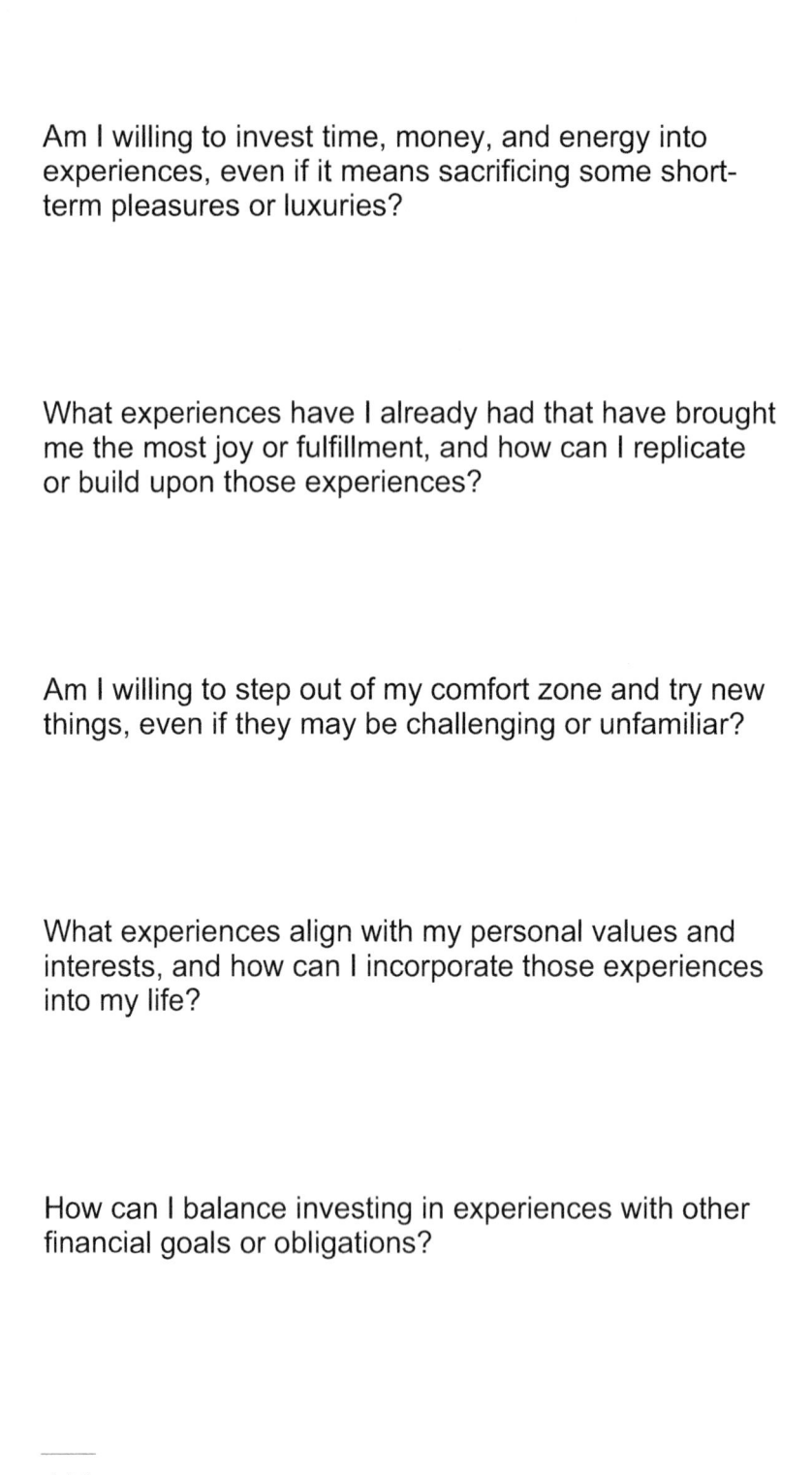

Am I willing to invest time, money, and energy into experiences, even if it means sacrificing some short-term pleasures or luxuries?

What experiences have I already had that have brought me the most joy or fulfillment, and how can I replicate or build upon those experiences?

Am I willing to step out of my comfort zone and try new things, even if they may be challenging or unfamiliar?

What experiences align with my personal values and interests, and how can I incorporate those experiences into my life?

How can I balance investing in experiences with other financial goals or obligations?

How can I involve others, such as friends or family members, in the experiences I invest in, and how might that enhance the overall value of the experience?

How can I make intentional choices about investing in experiences, rather than simply reacting to external pressures or social expectations?

Savouring

Savouring is a powerful tool for increasing happiness in our lives. It involves **consciously stepping outside** of our own experience and reflecting on the positive aspects of a moment or event. There are several ways to enhance the experience of savouring. One way is to **share it with someone else**, by telling a friend or loved one about the experience. Another way is to **physically express your happiness** through jumping around, yelling, or laughing. These actions help to reinforce the positive emotions associated with the experience.

On the other hand, there are also several factors that can **decrease the experience of savouring**. For instance, **not being fully present in the moment** and constantly thinking about the future can detract from our ability to fully savour the experience. Additionally, **feeling like we don't deserve** the experience or that it will be over soon can also prevent us from fully enjoying it.

It's important to note that the **act of taking pictures** for Instagram, for example**, should not replace the real experience.** Instead, we should focus on truly experiencing and savouring the moment, and then maybe sharing it with others through pictures or words.

One exercise that can help enhance the experience of savouring is to **replay happy memories** in our minds **for eight minutes a day, for three days**. This exercise helps to reinforce positive memories and experiences in our minds, and makes it easier to savour similar experiences in the future.

Here are some questions someone might ask themselves about savouring:

What does it mean to savour a moment, experience, or emotion, and how can it contribute to greater happiness and well-being?

What are some experiences or moments in my life that I've savoured in the past, and how did that contribute to my overall happiness?

Am I generally able to slow down and appreciate the present moment, or do I tend to rush through experiences or focus on future goals?

What might be some barriers to my ability to savour experiences, such as distractions, stress, or negative thought patterns?

How can I cultivate a habit of savouring, such as by taking time to reflect on positive experiences, using mindfulness techniques, or expressing gratitude?

Are there particular types of experiences or moments that I find easiest or most rewarding to savour, and how can I incorporate more of those into my life?

How can I share the experience of savouring with others, such as by discussing positive experiences with friends or loved ones or taking time to appreciate natural beauty with others?

How can I use savouring as a tool for coping with difficult emotions or challenging situations, such as by finding small moments of joy or gratitude even in tough circumstances?

What can I learn about myself and my values by savouring positive experiences, and how can that contribute to greater self-awareness and personal growth?

How can I maintain a balance between savouring positive experiences and still moving forward and pursuing new goals and opportunities in my life?

Negative Visualization

Negative visualization is a powerful technique that can help individuals **cultivate gratitude, overcome fears and anxieties**, and enhance their overall well-being. It involves imagining the opposite of what we typically focus on and **visualizing what we would lose or miss out on** if we didn't have what we currently have in our lives. This practice can help **shift our perspective** and allow us to appreciate what we have instead of taking it for granted.

For example, if someone is struggling with a job that they dislike, they can use negative visualization to imagine what their life would be like if they didn't have that job. They might imagine the financial stress, the lack of purpose or direction, and the missed opportunities that would come with not having that job. By doing so, they may begin to appreciate their job more and feel a greater sense of gratitude for it.

Another aspect of negative visualization involves **imagining worst-case scenarios**. While this might seem counterintuitive to happiness, it can actually help individuals **prepare for potential setbacks and cope better** with unexpected challenges. By visualizing worst-case scenarios, we can develop a sense of resilience and inner strength that can help us navigate difficult situations with greater ease and grace.

However, it's important to note that negative visualization **should not be used as a way to dwell on negative thoughts** or to induce anxiety or fear. It's important to balance this technique with positive visualization and gratitude practices to maintain a

healthy perspective and avoid excessive rumination on negative outcomes.
Here is a practical example and guide for using negative visualization:

Negative visualization is a technique used to help individuals appreciate what they have and increase their gratitude by imagining a life without some of their most valued possessions or experiences. It involves visualizing the loss of something positive in your life, such as a loved one, a job, or a place, in order to increase your appreciation for what you have and develop a more positive outlook on life.

Here's a step-by-step guide for using it:

Set aside some quiet time for yourself. Find a comfortable and distraction-free environment where you can focus on your thoughts and feelings.

Choose a positive aspect of your life that you may be taking for granted, such as a person, a place, or an experience.

Imagine losing that positive aspect of your life. Visualize what it would be like to no longer have it, how it would impact your life, and how you would feel without it. Try to be as vivid and detailed as possible in your visualization.

Reflect on the emotions that come up for you during this exercise. Acknowledge any feelings of loss, sadness, or grief that may arise, but also try to focus on the positive aspects of your experience.

After finishing the visualization, take a few deep breaths and try to shift your focus back to the present moment. Notice any positive emotions that may arise as a result of this exercise, such as a greater sense of gratitude, appreciation, or contentment.

Repeat this exercise regularly, focusing on different positive aspects of your life each time. Over time, this practice can help you cultivate a greater sense of gratitude and appreciation for what you have, and help you develop a more positive outlook on life.

Remember that negative visualization is just one tool among many that can be used to cultivate gratitude and appreciation in your life. It's important to find a practice that works for you and to approach it with an open and curious mindset.

Gratitude

Gratitude is a powerful tool for increasing happiness and well-being. It is a way of recognizing and acknowledging the good things in our lives and feeling grateful for them. Here are some ways in which gratitude can help with being happy:

Better health

Studies have shown that people who practice gratitude have **better physical health**. They have **stronger immune systems**, lower blood pressure, and better **sleep** quality.

Focus on positive things

Gratitude helps to **shift our focus** from negative to positive things. It makes us more aware of the good things in our lives, and we start to notice and appreciate them more.

Sharing gratitude

Sharing gratitude with others is **even more powerful** than just feeling grateful on our own. Writing a gratitude letter to someone you appreciate and delivering it in person can have a significant impact on both you and the recipient.

Happiness lasts longer

When we **share our happiness** with others, it **tends to last longer**. The act of sharing our gratitude reinforces the positive feelings and helps us to hold on to them for longer.

Improve relationships

Practicing gratitude towards our partners, family, friends, or colleagues can **improve our relationships with them**. It helps us to see their positive qualities and feel more connected to them.

Boost team morale

In a work setting, showing appreciation towards team members can **boost morale and improve productivity**. When people **feel valued** and **appreciated**, they are more **motivated** to put in effort and work together effectively.

In summary, gratitude is a simple but powerful practice that can significantly impact our happiness and well-being.

You can find a downloadable gratitude journal on this page:
www.creativestartupacademy.com/resources-hf

Here are some gratitude exercises that you can try:

Gratitude Journaling

Write down 3-5 things that you are grateful for each day. Try to focus on specific details and experiences rather than generic statements.

Gratitude Letter

Write a letter to someone who has positively impacted your life and express your gratitude to them. Deliver the letter in person or through email if possible.

Gratitude Walk

Take a walk outside and intentionally focus on the things that you are grateful for in your surroundings. It could be the beauty of nature, the kindness of strangers, or the warmth of the sun on your skin.

Gratitude Meditation

Take a few minutes each day to sit in silence and focus on the things you are grateful for. You can repeat a mantra or simply visualize the things you are grateful for in your mind.

Gratitude Jar

Write down moments of gratitude on small pieces of paper and put them in a jar. Whenever you need a boost of positivity, read through the notes in the jar.

Gratitude Sharing

Share something you are grateful for with a friend, family member, or co-worker each day. It could be as simple as expressing your appreciation for their support or for something they did that day.

Gratitude Visualization

Take a few minutes each day to visualize something you are grateful for in great detail. Imagine the sights, sounds, and feelings associated with that experience.

Remember that gratitude exercises are just one tool among many that can be used to cultivate a greater sense of positivity and well-being in your life. Experiment with different exercises and find what works best for you.

Re-experiencing

Re-experiencing is a technique that involves **intentionally revisiting a past positive experience** in order to relive the emotions associated with it. It can be particularly helpful **for boosting happiness and well-being,** as it allows us to **savor positive experiences** and prolong the positive emotions they generate.

One common challenge with positive experiences is that they can **become less exciting or meaningful over time**, as we adapt to them and they become our new normal. This is known as the hedonic adaptation or **"hedonic treadmill"** effect. However, by intentionally re-experiencing the positive emotions associated with a past experience, we can help **counteract this effect** and maintain our appreciation and enjoyment of it.

To practice re-experiencing, start by **identifying a past positive experience** that you would like to revisit. This could be a vacation, a special event, a personal achievement, or any other experience that brought you joy or satisfaction. Then, take some time to reflect on the experience and try to recall as many details as possible, such as the sights, sounds, and feelings you experienced at the time.

Once you have a clear image of the experience in your mind, try to **recreate the emotions** you felt at the time. You can do this by imagining yourself back in that moment, or by using sensory cues such as photos, music, or scents that remind you of the experience. Allow yourself to fully immerse in the positive emotions, and try to **savor the experience** as though you were reliving it in the present.

Re-experiencing can also be a helpful tool for shifting your perspective and cultivating gratitude. By intentionally revisiting past positive experiences, we can **remind ourselves of the good things in our lives and appreciate them more fully**. Additionally, by sharing these experiences with others, we can **strengthen our social connections** and increase our overall sense of well-being.

Concretely observing

Concretely observing your situation and finding a **reference point that is not as good as yours can help increase happiness.** Sometimes, we can get lost in negative thinking and lose sight of the good things in our lives. By actively looking for a reference point that is less fortunate, we can **gain perspective** and appreciate what we have.

For example, if you are feeling down about your job, you can think about someone who is currently unemployed and struggling to make ends meet. By comparing your situation to theirs, you may realize that you have job security, a steady income, and opportunities for growth that they do not have. This can help you appreciate your job and feel more grateful for it.

It's important to note that concretely observing your situation **does not mean denying or ignoring your feelings** of dissatisfaction or unhappiness. It simply means taking a step back to gain perspective and look at the bigger picture. By doing this, you can shift your focus from what you don't have to what you do have, which can lead to greater happiness and contentment.

Here are some questions that help you with that:

What are some good things in my life that I tend to take for granted?

How does my current situation compare to those who are less fortunate than me?

What are some specific things that I can do to appreciate what I have more?

How can I shift my focus from negative thinking to positive thinking?

What are some examples of people or situations that inspire me to be more grateful?

How can I use my experiences to help others who may be struggling?

What are some small changes I can make in my daily routine to help me appreciate what I have?

How can I cultivate a mindset of gratitude and appreciation in my life?

What are some simple things I can do to remind myself of the good things in my life?

How can I use my privilege or advantages to help others who may be less fortunate than me?

Interrupt consumption

Interrupting your consumption can have a significant impact on your happiness. When we consume things, whether it's food, TV shows, or other experiences, we **often start to lose interest or enjoyment over time.** This is because we become **habituated** to the experience, and it no longer provides the same level of novelty or stimulation as it did at first.

By interrupting your consumption, you **break this habituation process and introduce new reference points.** For example, if you're eating a hot dog, taking a break from eating it and then coming back to it later can make it taste even better. Similarly, if you're watching a TV show, pausing it and watching a commercial for another show can increase your enjoyment of both shows.

Interrupting your consumption can also help you **appreciate the good things in your life more.** By spacing out enjoyable experiences and avoiding overindulging in them, you can prevent yourself from becoming bored or desensitized to them. For example, if you eat the same ice cream flavor every day, you may start to lose interest in it. But if you switch up your flavors and come back to your favorite flavor later, it will taste much better.

Overall, interrupting your consumption can help you increase your variety, appreciate the good things in your life more, and introduce new reference points to make experiences more enjoyable.

Answer the following questions:

How much time do I spend consuming things, such as food, TV shows, or other experiences?

How often do I feel bored or dissatisfied with my consumption habits?

What are some signs that I may be becoming habituated to my consumption habits?

What are some alternative activities that I can engage in instead of consuming things?

How can I become more mindful of my consumption habits and their impact on my happiness?

What are some strategies I can use to interrupt my consumption habits and increase novelty and stimulation?

How can I balance my desire for novelty and stimulation with my need for rest and relaxation?
What are some ways that I can make my consumption habits more intentional?

Wanting the right part

Research has shown **that identifying and utilizing our signature strengths** can lead to increased happiness and well-being. Signature strengths are those character strengths that are **most essential** to who we are as individuals.

One way to activate your signature strengths is to seek out jobs or career paths that allow you to **use them on a regular basis.** This can help create a sense of purpose and satisfaction in your work, leading to greater happiness overall.

Additionally, you can try using your signature strengths in new and **creative ways each day for a week**. This can help reduce feelings of depression and increase happiness for up to six months or longer, according to studies.

The sweet spot for utilizing signature strengths in your job seems to be **using four of your seven strengths regularly.** This can create a positive work environment and improve job satisfaction.

So, by identifying and utilizing your signature strengths, you can find more meaning and happiness in your work and daily life.

Let's take a look at the following questions:

What are my signature strengths, and how can I identify them?

In what ways have I utilized my signature strengths in the past, and how have they contributed to my happiness and well-being?

How can I intentionally incorporate my signature strengths into my daily life, both at work and at home?

How can I leverage my signature strengths to overcome challenges or obstacles that I encounter in my life?

How can I use my signature strengths to contribute to the well-being of others, and to make a positive impact on the world around me?

How can I develop new skills or talents that complement my signature strengths, and help me to achieve even greater happiness and success?

What are some potential barriers or challenges that I may face in utilizing my signature strengths, and how can I overcome them?

How can I continue to grow and develop my signature strengths over time, and use them to achieve my long-term goals and aspirations?

What are some potential blind spots or weaknesses that I should be aware of as I focus on leveraging my signature strengths, and how can I address them?

How can I use my knowledge of my signature strengths to build stronger relationships with others, and to connect more deeply with the people and communities around me?

Flow

Flow is a state of mind that occurs when a person is **fully immersed in an activity that is both challenging and attainable,** resulting in a feeling of intense **focus**, **engagement**, and **enjoyment**. The concept of flow was first introduced by psychologist **Mihaly Csikszentmihalyi**, who studied people's subjective experiences during activities such as playing music, painting, or rock climbing.

Flow is characterized by a number of **key features**. The activity must be **challenging, but not so difficult** that it is impossible to complete. The individual must also have a **strong sense of focus** and concentration, with all attention directed towards the task at hand. The activity itself must be **intrinsically rewarding**, meaning that the individual finds the task enjoyable and fulfilling.

When a person is in a state of flow, they often report feelings of **serenity** and a **loss of self-consciousness**. They **may lose track of time** passing and become unaware of their physical needs, such as hunger or fatigue. The activity becomes the primary focus of their attention, and they are **completely absorbed** in the process of performing it.

Flow can be experienced in a wide range of activities, from creative pursuits like painting or writing, to athletic activities like running or dancing, to intellectual pursuits like solving a complex problem. It is a state that **can be cultivated with practice**, and can lead to increased happiness, fulfillment, and a sense of achievement.

Activities that may lead to flow can be anything from sports and exercise, to creative pursuits like writing or painting, to work-related tasks. The key is to find an activity that you enjoy and are passionate about, and that also challenges you in a way that is not too overwhelming or too easy.

Go through these questions to discover more about yourself and being in flow:

What activities or tasks bring me into a state of flow, where I lose track of time and become fully immersed in the present moment?

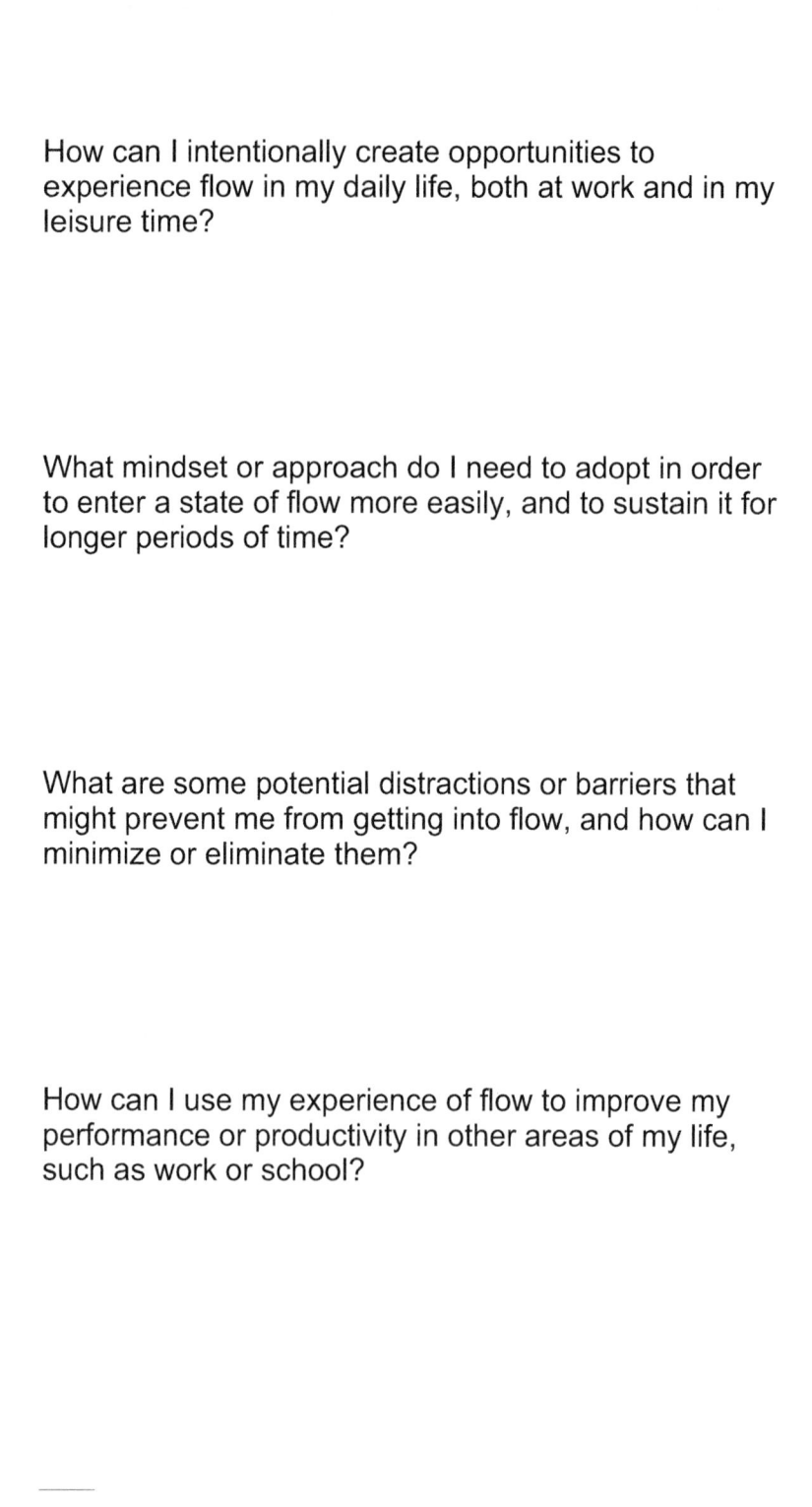

How can I intentionally create opportunities to experience flow in my daily life, both at work and in my leisure time?

What mindset or approach do I need to adopt in order to enter a state of flow more easily, and to sustain it for longer periods of time?

What are some potential distractions or barriers that might prevent me from getting into flow, and how can I minimize or eliminate them?

How can I use my experience of flow to improve my performance or productivity in other areas of my life, such as work or school?

How can I balance the demands of challenging tasks with my own skill level, in order to maximize my chances of entering a state of flow?

How can I use my experience of flow to cultivate a greater sense of purpose or meaning in my life, and to feel more fulfilled and satisfied with my accomplishments?

How can I recognize when I am in a state of flow, and use this awareness to deepen my focus and engagement with the task at hand?

How can I use my experience of flow to build stronger connections with others, and to contribute to a greater sense of teamwork or collaboration?

What are some potential downsides or risks associated with being in a state of flow, and how can I manage these effectively in order to maintain my well-being and avoid burnout?

Kindness

Research has shown that engaging in acts of kindness can **increase our overall level of happiness**. When we perform acts of kindness, such as doing something nice for a friend or stranger, our brain releases **feel-good chemicals** like oxytocin and dopamine. This can lead to a positive mood and a greater sense of well-being.

Interestingly, studies have found that performing **multiple acts of kindness** per day can have an even greater impact on our happiness than just doing one or two. This may be because the more we engage in these behaviors, the more they become ingrained as part of our daily routine and the more we feel connected to others.

Additionally, research has found that **spending money on others** can lead to greater happiness than spending it on ourselves. This may be because when we spend money on others, we feel a sense of social connection and contribution to the world, which can boost our overall sense of well-being.

In summary, wanting better things for ourselves can sometimes lead to a never-ending cycle of desire and dissatisfaction. But focusing on acts of kindness and spending money on others can shift our attention away from ourselves and towards the happiness of those around us.

Let's look at that in more detail with these questions:

What specific acts of kindness can I engage in today, both towards myself and others, in order to boost my mood and increase my overall level of happiness?

How can I cultivate a greater sense of empathy and compassion towards others, and use this as a motivation to engage in acts of kindness and generosity?

What are some potential barriers or obstacles that might prevent me from engaging in acts of kindness, and how can I overcome them?

How can I develop a regular practice of engaging in acts of kindness, in order to make it a natural and habitual part of my daily life?

How can I involve others in my acts of kindness, in order to create a sense of community and shared purpose around this practice?

How can I use my experience of engaging in acts of kindness to build stronger relationships with others, and to deepen my sense of connection and belonging?

What are some potential downsides or risks associated with engaging in acts of kindness, such as burnout or feeling taken advantage of, and how can I manage these effectively?

How can I use my experience of engaging in acts of kindness to contribute to a larger cause or mission, and to make a positive impact on the world around me?

How can I track my progress and success in engaging in acts of kindness, in order to maintain my motivation and momentum over time?

How can I use my experience of engaging in acts of kindness to cultivate a greater sense of gratitude, appreciation, and joy in my life, both for myself and for others?

Social connections

Social connections are crucial to our overall well-being and happiness. In fact, they matter more than we might initially think. Studies have shown that people with strong social connections are **less likely to experience premature death**, more likely to survive fatal illnesses, and less likely to fall prey to stress-related disorders.

The benefits of social connections go beyond just physical health. People with strong social ties are also **more resilient** in the face of life's challenges. They have a support system to rely on during difficult times, and they are less likely to experience feelings of loneliness or isolation.

One reason why social connections are so important is that they help us to feel a **sense of belonging and purpose.** When we are part of a group or community, we have a shared sense of identity and values, which can give us a sense of meaning and fulfillment.

Furthermore, social connections provide opportunities for positive interactions, such as laughter, support, and companionship. These interactions **can boost our mood** and help us to feel happier overall.

In today's fast-paced world, it can be easy to overlook the importance of social connections. However, it is important to make time for socializing and to prioritize building and maintaining relationships with others.

Whether it's spending time with friends and family, joining a club or organization, or volunteering in the community, investing in social connections can pay off

in many ways, including greater happiness and well-being.
Let's dive into some questions:

What specific social connections do I currently have in my life, and how do they contribute to my overall well-being and happiness?

How can I intentionally cultivate new social connections, both in my personal and professional life, in order to increase my overall level of happiness and fulfillment?

What are some potential barriers or obstacles that might prevent me from forming strong social connections, and how can I overcome them?

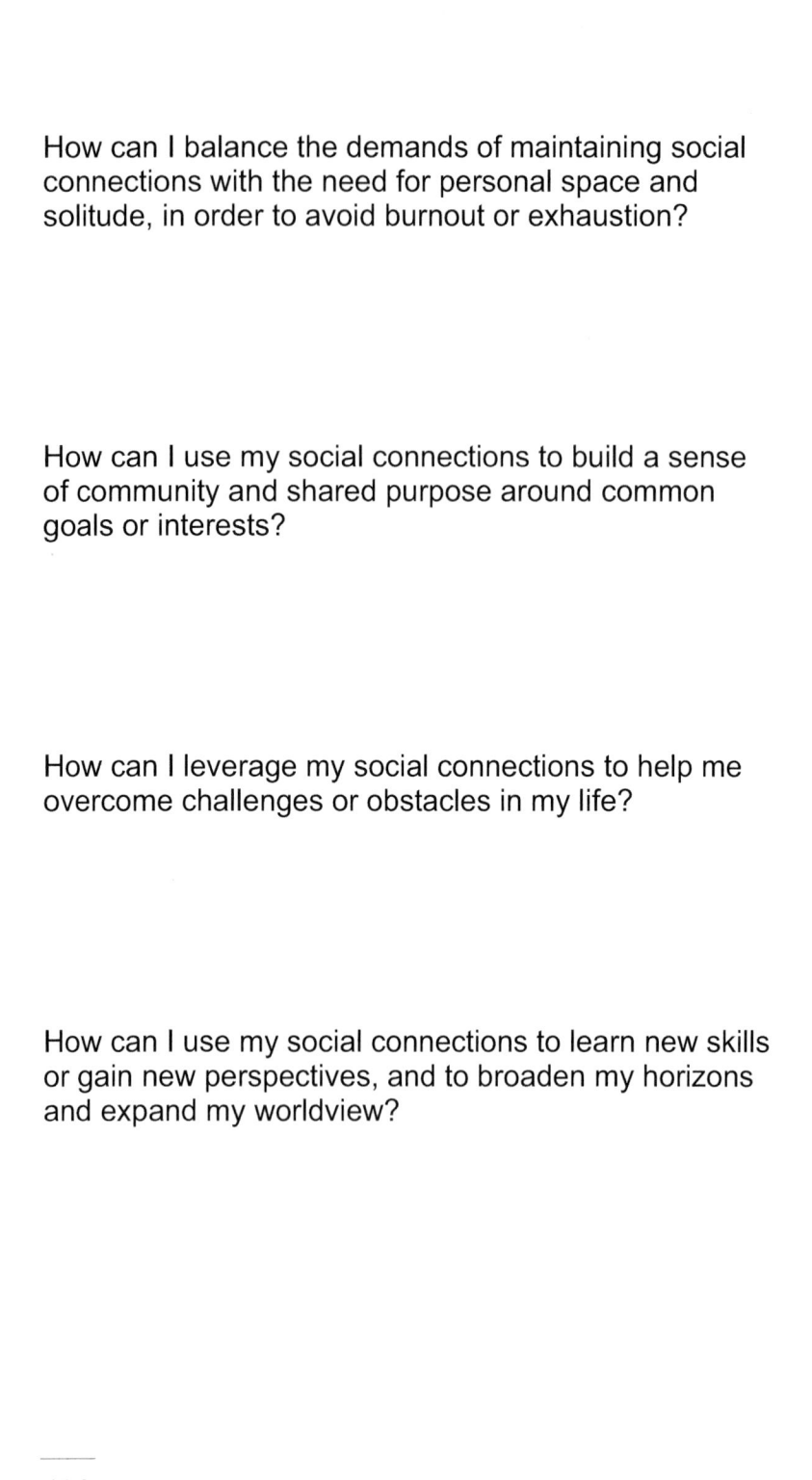

How can I balance the demands of maintaining social connections with the need for personal space and solitude, in order to avoid burnout or exhaustion?

How can I use my social connections to build a sense of community and shared purpose around common goals or interests?

How can I leverage my social connections to help me overcome challenges or obstacles in my life?

How can I use my social connections to learn new skills or gain new perspectives, and to broaden my horizons and expand my worldview?

How can I use my experience of building strong social connections to contribute to a larger cause or mission, and to make a positive impact on the world around me?

What are some potential downsides or risks associated with social connections, such as conflict or negative influence, and how can I manage these effectively?

Do something with others

Doing something with others can make an event more enjoyable for several reasons. Firstly, it provides a **sense of social connection** and **belonging**, which is a fundamental human need. When we engage in activities with others, we feel like we are a part of something, and this can increase our feelings of happiness and well-being.

Secondly, doing something with others can provide us with **new experiences and perspectives** that we may not have had otherwise. When we share an experience with someone else, we can learn from their insights and gain a new appreciation for the activity.

However, many people may not engage in social activities due to certain misconceptions. For example, they may believe that they would be happier alone instead of engaging in social connections. This belief is often untrue, as research has consistently shown that social connections are crucial to our well-being.

Additionally, people may think that others do not want to talk to them or spend time with them, leading to feelings of **social isolation and loneliness**. However, this belief is often based on negative self-talk and is not necessarily reflective of reality. Most people are open to social connections and are willing to engage in activities with others.

In summary, engaging in social activities with others can significantly increase our happiness and well-being. It is essential to **challenge any negative self-talk and misconceptions** that may prevent us from engaging in social connections and to prioritize spending time with others.

Some questions for you:

What are some examples of activities that are more enjoyable when done with others?

What are some benefits of engaging in group activities?

How can group activities enhance our personal growth and development?

What are some ways to overcome social anxiety and connect with others during group activities?

How does participating in group activities help build teamwork and collaboration skills?

What are some challenges that can arise when doing things with others, and how can they be addressed?

How can we ensure that everyone feels included and valued during group activities?

How can we balance our own preferences and needs with those of the group when planning and participating in activities together?

How can we use group activities to build and strengthen relationships with others?

Mind Control

Mind control refers to the ability to **consciously direct one's own thoughts and focus on specific tasks or goals**. It involves being aware of and regulating one's own mental processes to **maintain concentration** and prevent distractions. Mind control can be a valuable skill in many areas of life, including work, sports, and personal relationships.

One common obstacle to achieving mind control is **mind wandering**, which can lead to reduced productivity and increased stress. Mind wandering occurs when our thoughts drift away from the task at hand and become focused on unrelated or irrelevant matters. This can happen when we are bored, distracted, or simply not fully engaged in the task we are doing.

To improve mind control, it is important to **be aware of when our minds are wandering** and to take steps to refocus our attention. This can involve techniques such as mindfulness meditation, where one learns to observe their own thoughts without judgment and bring their focus back to the present moment.

Other strategies for improving mind control include **setting clear goals** and prioritizing tasks, breaking large tasks into smaller, more manageable steps, and avoiding multitasking as much as possible.

I also prepared some questions for you to understand yourself better and when your mind wonders:

How well do I feel that I can focus my thoughts and control my attention when needed?

What are some of the specific strategies or techniques that I use to maintain focus and stay on task, and how effective do I find them?

Are there any particular types of tasks or situations where I struggle to maintain focus and control my thoughts, and what might be some reasons for this?

How much of my ability to control my thoughts and focus on tasks is influenced by external factors, such as distractions, stress, or other people's expectations? Are there any specific habits or behaviors that I engage in that interfere with my ability to control my thoughts and focus on tasks, and how might I change these behaviors?

How do my emotions and mood affect my ability to control my thoughts and focus on tasks, and what can I do to manage these factors more effectively?

How can I set goals and priorities that align with my values and motivations, and use these to guide my thoughts and actions in a more intentional way?

How can I cultivate greater awareness and mindfulness in my daily life, in order to better control my thoughts and stay focused on the present moment?

Are there any particular areas of my life where I would like to improve my ability to control my thoughts and focus on goals, and what steps can I take to work towards these improvements?

How can I use my ability to control my thoughts and focus on goals in a way that is aligned with my values and contributes to my overall well-being and sense of purpose?

Meditation

Meditation is one effective way to **reduce mind wandering** and improve focus on the present moment. It involves training the mind to stay in the present moment and to let go of distractions, such as thoughts about the past or future.

As previously mentioned, studies have shown that regular meditation practice can lead to **structural changes in the brain,** including increased gray matter in regions involved in attention, emotional regulation, and self-awareness. Additionally, loving-kindness meditation, which involves generating feelings of love and kindness towards oneself and others, has been found to **increase positive emotions and social connections.**

Other techniques that can help reduce mind wandering include setting clear goals, breaking tasks into smaller, more manageable chunks, practicing mindfulness in daily activities, and limiting distractions like electronic devices. Regular **exercise**, good **sleep hygiene**, and a healthy **diet** can also help improve **focus** and reduce mind wandering.

Go through the following questions to explore more:

How often do I find my mind wandering or engaging in spontaneous thoughts, and what might be some common triggers or patterns for this type of thinking?

Are there any particular activities or situations where I find my mind wandering more frequently or intensely, and what might be some reasons for this?

How do my patterns of mind-wandering or spontaneous thinking affect my overall well-being, productivity, and sense of purpose in life?

How can I strike a balance between allowing my mind to wander and engage in creative thinking, while also staying focused and productive when necessary?

How do external factors, such as stress, distractions, or technology, impact my tendency to engage in mind-wandering or spontaneous thinking?

How can I use mindfulness practices or other techniques to become more aware of my mind-wandering patterns and learn to control them more effectively?

Are there any particular areas of my life, such as work or relationships, where my mind-wandering might be interfering with my ability to achieve my goals or meet my responsibilities?

How can I use my tendency towards spontaneous thinking to my advantage, such as by engaging in creative thinking or problem-solving?

How can I use my knowledge of my mind-wandering tendencies to better understand my own thinking patterns and tendencies, and work towards developing a more intentional and purposeful mindset?

You can find meditations on this page:
www.creativestartupacademy.com/resources-hf

Seeing good things

Seeing the good things and making them visible can have a positive impact on our happiness. When we surround ourselves **with reminders of positive experiences and accomplishments**, we are more likely to engage in positive behaviors and thoughts.

I mentioned it before, but want to repeat it here: One way to do this is through **gratitude practice**, where we intentionally focus on the good things in our lives and express gratitude for them. This can be done through journaling, making a list of things we're grateful for, or simply reflecting on positive experiences.

In addition to gratitude practice, we can also surround ourselves with **positive affirmations** and reminders of our strengths and accomplishments. This can be done through **visual** cues such as sticky notes or posters with positive messages, or even **wearing clothing or accessories that remind us of positive experiences** or qualities we possess.

By making the **good things visible** and regularly reminding ourselves of them, we can cultivate a more positive and optimistic mindset, which in turn contributes to our overall happiness and well-being.

Let's look into this in more detail:

What are some positive experiences that I've had recently, and how can I make them visible in my surroundings?

How can I actively seek out and notice the good things in my life, and how might this impact my overall happiness?

In what ways can I celebrate my accomplishments and successes, and how might this boost my motivation and confidence?

How can I incorporate more reminders of positivity and gratitude into my daily routine, and what specific actions can I take to make this happen?

What are some negative thought patterns or behaviors that I engage in, and how might focusing on positive experiences help me to counteract these tendencies?

How can I cultivate a mindset of gratitude and appreciation, and what strategies can I use to make this a consistent habit?

What role do my surroundings and environment play in shaping my mood and outlook, and how can I create a space that is conducive to positivity and happiness?

How might sharing positive experiences and accomplishments with others enhance my own happiness and well-being?

In what ways can I actively seek out opportunities to experience new and positive things, and how might this impact my overall happiness and fulfillment?

What are some small, everyday actions that I can take to remind myself of the good things in my life and cultivate a more positive outlook?

Goal setting

Setting goals can contribute significantly to our happiness by giving us a **sense of purpose, direction, and achievement.** Goals provide us with a framework for organizing our time and energy, and help us to focus our attention and efforts on specific tasks or outcomes.

When we set goals that are **meaningful and challenging**, we are more likely to experience a sense of accomplishment and satisfaction when we achieve them. This feeling of accomplishment can increase our self-esteem and sense of self-worth, which can in turn contribute to our overall happiness.

Furthermore, the process of setting and working towards goals can also provide us with a sense of **control** in our lives. By setting goals, we are actively taking steps to shape our own future and to **create the kind of life we want to live**. This sense of control can be empowering and can contribute to our overall sense of well-being.

It's important to note, however, that the type of goals we set can also impact our happiness. Goals that are too ambitious or unrealistic can lead to feelings of frustration or failure, while goals that are too easy may not provide enough of a challenge to create a **sense of achievement**. Additionally, goals that are **aligned with our personal values** and interests are more likely to bring us happiness than goals that are imposed upon us by others or that do not align with our authentic selves.

In summary, setting and working towards meaningful, challenging, and personally aligned goals can contribute to our happiness by providing us with a sense of purpose, achievement, and control over our lives.

Here is one way to set goals - using another acronym (I like those :-))
ACHIEVE
- As if now
- Clear and specific
- Hittable
- In a positive direction
- Exciting
- Value based
- Ecological

As if now

Phrase your goal **as a statement** of accomplishment rather than a wish. For instance, instead of saying "I want a successful company" or "I will have a successful company," say "I have a successful company." This helps shift your mindset and enables you to subconsciously work towards achieving it.

Clear and specific

Setting a goal without **specific details** is pointless because you cannot determine if you have achieved it. To ensure clarity, include details such as a date, location, and the people you want to achieve the goal with. Instead of stating a generic goal of having a "successful company," specify the type of successful company you want to create, including details such as turnover and staff size. By doing this, you can clarify your goal and understand the milestones you need to reach to achieve it. For example, instead of saying "I have a successful company," say "It is December 2029, and I have established a profitable web design company in Auckland, New Zealand, with five staff members, a business partner named (INSERT NAME), and an annual turnover of 500,000 NZD." This level of specificity provides a clear roadmap to achieving your goal.

Hittable

Ensure that your goal is **attainable** by evaluating your resources and timeline. Consider whether you have the necessary skills and resources to achieve it within the set timeframe. If not, identify what you need and re-evaluate the timeline accordingly. Assess the time you can realistically invest in achieving the goal, taking into account other commitments such as work. Approach your goal from a practical standpoint to ensure that it is achievable.

In a positive direction

When phrasing your goal, focus on expressing it positively. Instead of stating what you don't want, **focus on what you do want to achieve**. For instance, instead of saying "I don't want to be employed full-time," say "I have a profitable web design company" to emphasize what you want to achieve. This helps to keep your mind focused on the positive outcome and motivates you towards achieving it.

Exciting

Your goal should be **personally motivating and exciting** to you. As I mentioned earlier, it should be your own goal, not someone else's, as this is crucial for maintaining motivation. Take a look at the goal you have written down and ask yourself if it excites you. Will you be thrilled once you achieve it? If the answer is "No," consider rephrasing it or finding a new goal that truly excites and motivates you. Remember, setting a goal that sparks your passion and interest will give you the drive to pursue it with enthusiasm and determination.

Value based

Setting goals that **align with your personal values** is crucial for achieving long-term happiness and fulfillment. When you set goals that are based on your values, you are more likely to be motivated and committed to achieving them, as they are connected to what truly matters to you. Additionally, achieving value-based goals can give you a sense of purpose and meaning in your life, which can boost your overall well-being and satisfaction. By setting value-based goals, you can create a **clear direction** for your life that is in line with your beliefs and principles, leading to a more fulfilling and happy life.

Ecological

Consider the ecological impact of your goals by examining how they will **affect your environment** beyond just material possessions, such as money and living arrangements. This also includes how your goals will impact the **people** in your life, such as your **friends** and **family**. For instance, if your goal involves moving to a different country, you should consider the potential consequences for your loved ones. Are they comfortable with your decision to move, or do they have concerns? It is important to reflect on these ecological factors and weigh the potential impact of your goals on your relationships and community.

Try it out. Write your goal here using the ACHIEVE acronym:

Implementation intention

Implementation intention is **a self-regulation strategy** that involves planning a specific response to a potential situational cue or trigger that might otherwise derail our progress towards a goal. By making a **clear plan** of what to do in certain situations, we are more likely to stick to our goals and achieve them.

The basic structure of an implementation intention **is "if-then" planning**. The if-then statement helps to create a clear link between a situational cue and a specific response. This can be especially helpful for automatic behaviors or habits, where we may not even realize we are making a decision.

Research has shown that implementation intentions can **lead to better goal attainment** in a variety of domains, including health, academic performance, and work productivity. By setting specific plans for how to respond to situational cues, we can overcome obstacles and stay on track towards our goals.

One example of an implementation intention exercise is to **write down a goal** and then **list potential obstacles** that could get in the way. Then, for each obstacle, come up with an **if-then plan** for how to respond. This can help to prepare you for potential challenges and keep you focused on your goal.

Here are some more questions for you to answer:

What are some potential obstacles that could prevent me from achieving my goal?

Are there any internal barriers, such as negative self-talk or limiting beliefs, that could hold me back?

How can I address these obstacles or barriers?

What specific actions can I take to overcome these obstacles and achieve my goal?

What resources or support do I need to help me achieve my goal?

How will I measure my progress and know when I have achieved my goal?

What is my timeline for achieving my goal?

How will I celebrate and reward myself once I have achieved my goal?

How can I stay motivated and committed to my goal, even when faced with challenges or setbacks?

WOOP

WOOP (Wish, Outcome, Obstacle, Plan) is a practical and effective **mental strategy** for achieving goals and fulfilling desires. It was developed by psychologist **Gabriele Oettingen** as a way to enhance motivation and goal achievement.

The four steps of WOOP are:

Wish

Identify your wish or goal, and be specific about what you want to achieve. This step helps you to focus on what you really want and clarify your intentions.

Why is this wish important to me?
How will achieving this wish benefit me?
How will you measure my progress towards achieving this wish?
Who can support me in achieving this wish?

Outcome

Imagine the **best possible outcome** of achieving your wish. Visualize it as vividly as possible and connect with the positive emotions associated with it. This step helps you to become motivated and excited about achieving your goal.

What would achieving my wish look like?
How would my life change if I achieved my wish?
How would I feel once you achieved my wish?
Who would benefit from me achieving my wish?

How would my relationships be affected by my achieving my wish?
What positive emotions would I experience when I achieve your wish?
Can I describe a specific scenario where I am living out of my wish?

Obstacle

Identify potential obstacles that might prevent you from achieving your goal. It could be an internal obstacle, such as a lack of confidence or motivation, or an external obstacle, such as time constraints or financial limitations.

What are some possible internal obstacles that might prevent me from achieving my goal?
How can I overcome these internal obstacles?
What are some external obstacles that might prevent me from achieving my goal?
How can I mitigate these external obstacles?
Have I encountered any obstacles in the past that have prevented me from achieving similar goals?
How did I overcome these obstacles?
Are there any resources or support systems I can utilize to help overcome potential obstacles?
How can I break down larger obstacles into smaller, more manageable tasks?
How can I prepare for potential obstacles before they occur?

Plan

Develop an if/then plan to overcome the obstacles and achieve your goal. The plan should be specific and actionable, such as "If I encounter obstacle X, then I will do Y." This step helps you to be prepared for obstacles and to create a concrete plan for achieving your goal.

Write your if/then plan down here for the goal that you have set yourself earlier:

Research has shown that WOOP can be an effective strategy for **enhancing motivation**, goal attainment, and well-being. By visualizing positive outcomes and preparing for potential obstacles, individuals can increase their chances of successfully achieving their goals.

An example of using WOOP for a goal of regular exercise might be:

Wish: I wish to exercise for 30 minutes every day.

Outcome: If I exercise every day, I will feel more energized, improve my physical health, and feel proud of myself.

Obstacle: One potential obstacle could be feeling too tired or busy to exercise.

Plan: If I feel too tired or busy, then I will do a shorter workout or take a walk instead.

Learn About the Models

Learn about models

The **L in SMILE** stands for learning about the models. Here we explore some of the happiness models and techniques that have proven to contribute to happiness. Are you ready?

Happiness models

Happiness models **are frameworks or theories** that attempt to explain what happiness is, how it is achieved, and how it can be sustained. These models may be **based on research, personal experiences, or philosophical ideas** about human nature and well-being.

There are **several different happiness models**, each with its own perspective and approach. One common model is the subjective well-being model, which emphasizes the **importance of positive emotions**, life **satisfaction**, and a sense of **purpose or meaning** in life. Another model is the **PERMA model**, developed by positive psychologist **Martin Seligman**, which includes **five elements** that contribute to well-being: positive emotions, engagement, relationships, meaning, and accomplishment.

Other happiness models include the **hedonic model,** which focuses on pleasure and enjoyment, and the **eudaimonic model**, which emphasizes self-realization and personal growth. Some models also incorporate the role of external factors such as social support, economic conditions, and cultural norms.

Overall, happiness models aim to provide a framework for understanding what happiness means, how it can be achieved, and how it can be sustained over time. By identifying the key components of well-being, these models can help individuals and communities make choices that promote happiness and improve quality of life. Let's look at them in more detail.

PERMA

The PERMA model is a well-known model of happiness and well-being developed by positive psychology founder **Martin Seligman**. The model includes **five key elements** that contribute to human flourishing and happiness:

Positive emotions (P)

This includes feelings of joy, gratitude, serenity, interest, and other positive emotions that contribute to well-being.

Engagement (E)

This refers to being fully immersed in activities that we enjoy and that use our skills and strengths. When we experience engagement, we often lose track of time and feel a sense of flow.

Relationships (R)

Our social connections and relationships with others are crucial for our happiness and well-being. This includes having strong connections with family, friends, colleagues, and other social groups.

Meaning (M)

Having a sense of purpose and meaning in life is important for our happiness. This can come from contributing to society, working toward important goals, or engaging in activities that align with our values.

Accomplishment (A)

Achieving goals and feeling a sense of accomplishment is also important for our happiness. This includes achieving personal goals, mastering skills, and feeling a sense of competence.

5 ways of wellbeing

The 5 Ways to Wellbeing is a framework developed by the **New Economics Foundation (NEF)** in the **United Kingdom** to promote mental wellbeing. It is based on extensive research and suggests five key actions that individuals can take to improve their mental health and overall wellbeing.

Connect

Connect with the people around you, such as family, friends, colleagues, and neighbours. Building strong, positive relationships is essential for good mental health.

Be active

Regular physical activity is not only good for our physical health but also helps to boost our mood and reduce stress and anxiety. It doesn't have to be strenuous exercise; even simple activities such as walking, cycling, or gardening can make a difference.

Take notice

Pay attention to the present moment and the world around you. Take the time to notice the beauty of nature, savour the taste of food, or simply be mindful of your breathing. Being more aware of your thoughts and feelings can help you to better understand yourself and your reactions.

Keep learning

Learning new things can boost our self-esteem and increase our sense of purpose. It can be anything from taking a course, reading a book, or learning a new skill. Keeping your brain active is an essential part of good mental health.

Give

Doing something kind for someone else can boost our mood and increase our sense of connection to others. It can be as simple as offering a kind word or helping someone with a task. Giving can help us to feel good about ourselves and make a positive impact on the world around us.

10 keys to happier living

The 10 Keys to Happier Living is a framework for happiness and wellbeing developed by **Action for Happiness**, a UK-based non-profit organization. The framework is based on the latest scientific research and aims to provide practical tips for improving our overall wellbeing and leading a happier life.

The 10 Keys to Happier Living are:

Giving

Do things for others. Caring about others is fundamental to our happiness.

Relating

Connect with people. Relationships are the most important overall contributor to happiness.

Exercising

Take care of your body. Physical activity makes you feel good.

Awareness

Live life mindfully. Be aware of the world around you and what you are feeling.

Trying out

Keep learning new things. Learning new things keeps us curious and engaged.

Direction

Have goals to look forward to. Feeling good about the future is important for our happiness.

Resilience

Find ways to bounce back. Being resilient helps us cope with the challenges that life throws at us.

Emotions

Take a positive approach. Positive emotions - like joy, gratitude, contentment, inspiration - broaden our thinking and build our resources.

Acceptance

Be comfortable with who you are. Accepting yourself, warts and all, helps you to feel good about yourself and build resilience.

Meaning

Be part of something bigger. People who have meaning and purpose in their lives are happier, feel more in control and get more out of what they do.

These 10 keys are not a strict prescription for happiness, but rather a guide to help people focus on the areas of life that are important for wellbeing.

GNH

The concept of **Gross National Happiness (GNH)** was first introduced in **Bhutan** in **1972** by **King Jigme Singye Wangchuck** as a way to measure the country's progress and development beyond just economic growth. The idea was to prioritize the happiness and wellbeing of citizens, rather than solely focusing on GDP.

The GNH model identifies nine domains that contribute to overall happiness and wellbeing:

Psychological wellbeing

This domain is concerned with mental and emotional wellbeing, including feelings of contentment, joy, and peace of mind.

Health

This domain includes physical health, access to healthcare, and the ability to lead a healthy lifestyle.

Education

This domain emphasizes the importance of education and lifelong learning for personal growth and development.

Cultural diversity and resilience

This domain acknowledges the importance of preserving and celebrating cultural diversity, as well as promoting resilience in the face of cultural and environmental challenges.

Time use

This domain emphasizes the importance of using time in meaningful and fulfilling ways, such as pursuing hobbies, spending time with loved ones, and engaging in community activities.

Community vitality

This domain includes social connections, sense of community, and engagement in civic life.

Ecological diversity and resilience

This domain acknowledges the importance of preserving and protecting the natural environment for future generations.

Living standards

This domain includes basic needs such as access to housing, food, and clean water, as well as the ability to lead a comfortable and secure life.

Governance

This domain emphasizes the importance of effective and transparent governance, as well as promoting democratic values and human rights.

Mindfulness

Mindfulness is the practice of **bringing your attention to the present moment** and **accepting it without judgment**. It's about being fully engaged and present in what you're doing, rather than being distracted by worries about the past or future.

Research has shown that mindfulness can have **numerous benefits for mental health and wellbeing**. For example, it can help reduce stress, anxiety, and depression, and improve overall feelings of happiness and contentment.

One of the ways that mindfulness can help with happiness is by allowing you to **fully engage with your experiences and appreciate the positive moments** in your life. When you're not distracted by worries or regrets, you're able to fully enjoy and **savor** the good things that happen to you.

Additionally, mindfulness can help you **cultivate a sense of acceptance** and non-judgment toward yourself and others. By accepting your thoughts and feelings without judging them, you can reduce feelings of self-criticism and increase self-compassion.

Overall, mindfulness is a powerful tool for increasing happiness and wellbeing, as it allows you to be fully present and engaged with your life, while also fostering a sense of acceptance and compassion toward yourself and others.

ABC model

The ABC model is a **cognitive-behavioral therapy technique** used to identify and change negative thought patterns. The model suggests that events or situations (A) do not directly cause our emotional and behavioral responses (C). Rather, it is our beliefs or thoughts (B) about the events or situations that lead to our emotional and behavioral responses.

Mindfulness meditation can be used in conjunction with the ABC model to help individuals become more aware of their thoughts and beliefs, and to challenge and change negative thought patterns. Through mindfulness meditation, individuals learn to observe their thoughts without judgment, and to become more aware of how their thoughts and beliefs impact their emotions and behaviors.

By practicing mindfulness meditation regularly, individuals can become more mindful in their daily lives, which can lead to greater awareness of negative thought patterns and the ability to challenge and change them.

In summary, the ABC model and mindfulness meditation can be powerful tools in promoting happiness and well-being by helping individuals become more aware of and change negative thought patterns.

Reflection Rose, Bud, Thorn

"Reflection Rose, Bud, Thorn" is a **simple and effective mindfulness practice** that can help you **reflect on your day** and gain **insights** into your thoughts, feelings, and experiences.

Here's how it works:

Reflection Rose

Visualize a rose in your mind's eye, and imagine that the petals of the rose represent different aspects of your day. Take a few moments to reflect on the events of your day, and assign each event to a specific petal of the rose. For example, one petal could represent a conversation you had with a friend, while another petal could represent a project you worked on at work.

Reflection Bud

Imagine a bud growing on the stem of the rose, and assign it a positive experience or insight from your day. This could be something you learned, something that made you happy, or something that inspired you.

Reflection Thorn

Finally, imagine a thorn on the stem of the rose, and assign it a negative experience or challenge from your day. This could be something that frustrated you, something that upset you, or something that you struggled with.

By reflecting on your day in this way, you can gain a greater sense of perspective and awareness about your experiences. You may also notice patterns or themes emerging over time, which can help you identify areas of your life that may need more attention or focus. Ultimately, the practice of "Reflection Rose, Bud, Thorn" can help you cultivate mindfulness, gratitude, and self-awareness.

Dr. Kristin Neff - Three Pillars of Self-Compassion

Dr. Kristin Neff is a well-known **researcher, psychologist**, and **author** who has contributed significantly to the field of self-compassion. She is a **pioneer** in the **study of self-compassion** and has developed a **widely-used scale for measuring it**. Her work has been instrumental in helping individuals to understand the importance of self-compassion and how to cultivate it in their lives. Dr. Neff has identified **three pillars of self-compassion** that are essential to its practice:

Self-kindness

Self-kindness is the first pillar of self-compassion. It involves **being warm, caring, and understanding** towards oneself, especially during times of difficulty or suffering. Self-kindness is about treating yourself with the same level of compassion and understanding that you would extend to a dear friend who was struggling.

Common humanity

The second pillar of self-compassion is common humanity. This involves **recognizing that suffering and difficulty are a part of the human experience** and that you are not alone in your struggles. Rather than feeling isolated and disconnected from others, common humanity reminds us that we are all in this together.

Mindfulness

The third pillar of self-compassion is mindfulness. This involves **being present and aware of your thoughts**, feelings, and sensations without judgment. Mindfulness helps you to see your thoughts and emotions more clearly and with greater acceptance, which can reduce feelings of stress and anxiety.

Taken together, these three pillars form the foundation of self-compassion. By practicing self-kindness, recognizing our common humanity, and being mindful, we can develop greater self-compassion and resilience in the face of life's challenges. Dr. Neff's work has shown that practicing self-compassion can lead to greater emotional well-being, reduced anxiety and depression, and more positive relationships with others.

ACT

Acceptance and Commitment Therapy (ACT) is a type of **psychotherapy** that focuses on helping individuals develop **psychological flexibility** and improve their overall well-being. It was developed in the 1990s by **Steven Hayes** and his colleagues and has since gained popularity as an evidence-based treatment for a range of mental health conditions.

The three pillars of ACT are:

Acceptance

Acceptance is the first pillar of ACT and involves learning to **accept difficult emotions**, thoughts, and experiences without trying to avoid or control them. This is in contrast to traditional **cognitive-behavioral therapy (CBT)**, which aims to challenge and change negative thoughts and beliefs.

In ACT, acceptance is seen as a way to **reduce the struggle with painful experiences** and create more psychological flexibility. By accepting our experiences, we can learn to respond to them more effectively and in line with our values.

Cognitive Defusion

The second pillar of ACT is cognitive defusion, which **refers to the process of distancing ourselves from unhelpful thoughts and beliefs**. In other words, it's about learning to observe our thoughts without getting caught up in them.

Cognitive defusion exercises may include imagining thoughts on leaves floating down a stream or visualizing them written on a chalkboard that can be erased. By defusing from our thoughts, **we can reduce their impact on our behavior and emotions.**

Commitment to Values

The third pillar of ACT is commitment to values, which involves clarifying and committing to our personal values and using them as a guide for our behavior. **Values are different from goals** in that they are ongoing, whereas goals are often specific and measurable.

Values may include things like **family, community, personal growth, or spirituality**. By committing to our values, we can create a sense of purpose and meaning in our lives, even in the face of difficult experiences.

Overall, ACT is a unique and powerful approach to **psychotherapy** that focuses on developing **psychological flexibility** through acceptance, cognitive defusion, and commitment to values. It can be helpful for a range of mental health conditions, including anxiety, depression, and chronic pain.

Engage with Tools

Engage with tools

The last letter in **SMILE is the E** which stands for 'engage with tools'. In this section, we will be discussing various tools and techniques that can assist you in achieving the happiness that you both desire and deserve.

Meditation apps

Meditation apps provide users with **guided meditations** and other **exercises** to help cultivate mindfulness and **reduce stress**. **Headspace** is one of the most popular meditation apps, offering a variety of guided meditations, mindfulness exercises, and sleep sounds. **Calm** is another popular meditation app, with guided meditations, sleep stories, and breathing exercises. **Insight Timer** is a free app that offers guided meditations from a variety of teachers and traditions, as well as a timer for self-guided meditation.

Gratitude journaling

Gratitude journaling involves writing down **things you're grateful for each day**, which can help shift your focus towards the positive and increase feelings of happiness and contentment. The Gratitude app offers a simple, easy-to-use interface for daily gratitude journaling, with customizable reminders to help you remember to journal.

The Five Minute Journal is another popular gratitude journaling app, with prompts for morning and evening reflections and weekly challenges to help you stay engaged with your gratitude practice.

You can find a downloadable gratitude journal on this page:
www.creativestartupacademy.com/resources-hf

Non-to-do lists

A non-to-do list is a way to **prioritize self-care and set boundaries** by identifying things you won't do. **Todoist** is a popular app for managing to-do lists, and can also be used to create and manage your non-to-do list. **Trello** is another popular project management app that can be used to create non-to-do lists and track progress towards self-care goals.

You can find downloadable Non ToDo list templates on this page:
www.creativestartupacademy.com/resources-hf

Aromatherapy

Aromatherapy involves using **scents to promote relaxation and reduce stress**. The Aromatherapy app offers information about different scents and their benefits, as well as recipes for creating your own aromatherapy blends. **The Essential Oils Reference Guide app** provides detailed information about essential oils and their therapeutic properties, as well as recipes for blending and diffusing essential oils.

It is important to exercise **caution** when using essential oils, as they can cause **allergic reactions** or other adverse effects in some people. Before using any new essential oil, it is important to do a **patch test** on a small area of skin to see if you have an allergic reaction. Additionally, **certain essential oils should not be used by pregnant or nursing women**, young **children**, or people with certain **medical conditions**. Always consult with a **healthcare professional** before using essential oils, especially if you are unsure about their safety or have any concerns.

Mindful moments

Taking **short breaks** throughout the day to focus on the present moment can help reduce stress and increase happiness. **The Mindfulness app** offers guided meditations, breathing exercises, and other mindfulness tools to help you stay centered throughout the day. **The Smiling Mind** app provides free, guided meditations and mindfulness exercises designed specifically for children and young adults.

Gratitude visits

Gratitude visits involve **expressing your gratitude directly to another person**, which can increase feelings of connection and social support. **The Happify app** offers tools and exercises to help you cultivate gratitude, positive social connections, and overall well-being. **The Happier app** provides a platform for sharing and celebrating small moments of happiness and connection with others, and offers tools and exercises for cultivating a positive mindset.

These are just a few examples of the many apps and tools available to help promote happiness and well-being. By exploring different options and finding what works best for you, you can develop a personalized approach to enhancing your overall quality of life.

ACT Meditation

We talked about ACT in the previous chapters. ACT (Acceptance and Commitment Therapy) meditation is a type of mindfulness meditation that aims to help individuals connect with their values, become more aware of their thoughts and emotions, and develop psychological flexibility. It involves learning to accept one's thoughts and emotions, without judgment or attempts to change them, while committing to behaviors that align with one's values.

During ACT meditation, individuals are encouraged to **observe their thoughts and emotions** as they arise, without trying to push them away or dwell on them. The focus is on being present in the moment and developing a sense of self-awareness. By practicing this form of meditation, individuals can learn to better manage difficult thoughts and emotions, reduce stress and anxiety, and improve overall well-being.

ACT meditation can be practiced in a variety of settings, including formal meditation sessions, as well as in everyday life situations. It can be helpful for those struggling with anxiety, depression, or other mental health challenges, as well as for individuals who want to develop greater emotional awareness and resilience.

Here is an ACT meditation.
Begin by finding a comfortable seated position, either on a cushion or a chair with your feet flat on the floor. Close your eyes and take a few deep breaths, allowing yourself to settle into this moment.

Now bring your attention to your breath. Notice the sensation of the air moving in and out of your body. You might notice the rise and fall of your chest or the sensation of the air passing through your nostrils.

As you breathe in, silently say to yourself, "I am here." And as you breathe out, silently say to yourself, "I am present." Repeat this to yourself for a few breaths, allowing yourself to fully arrive in this moment.

Now, bring to mind an image of yourself taking the ACT. See yourself sitting calmly and confidently, moving through each section with ease. Visualize yourself answering each question with clarity and precision, feeling confident in your abilities.

As you hold this image in your mind, notice any thoughts or feelings that arise. Perhaps you feel a sense of anxiety or doubt. Acknowledge these feelings without judgment, and then let them go. Return your attention to the image of yourself performing well.

Now, bring to mind a sense of gratitude for your abilities and your opportunities. Take a moment to appreciate the hard work you've put in to prepare for this exam, and the support of those around you.

As you come to the end of this meditation, take a deep breath in and exhale slowly. When you're ready, gently open your eyes and return to your day, carrying with you a sense of calm and confidence.

You can find the recorded version of this meditation on this page:
www.creativestartupacademy.com/resources-hf

Reflective meditation

Reflective meditation, also known as **introspection or contemplative meditation**, involves reflecting on one's own thoughts and feelings to gain insight and understanding. This type of meditation can be helpful in cultivating self-awareness, developing emotional intelligence, and promoting happiness.

Reflective meditation can help with happiness in several ways. Firstly, by reflecting on one's thoughts and feelings, individuals can gain **insight into their own patterns of thinking and behavior**. This awareness can help them identify negative thought patterns and replace them with more positive ones, leading to a greater sense of well-being.

Secondly, reflective meditation can help individuals develop **empathy and compassion** towards themselves and others. By reflecting on their own experiences and emotions, individuals can gain a better understanding of the experiences and emotions of others, leading to greater empathy and a deeper connection with others.

Finally, reflective meditation can help individuals cultivate a **sense of gratitude and appreciation** for the present moment. By reflecting on the good things in their lives, individuals can shift their focus away from negative thoughts and feelings, leading to a more positive outlook and a greater sense of happiness.

To practice reflective meditation, find a quiet and comfortable place to sit and reflect on your thoughts and feelings. You can start by focusing on your breath and then gradually turn your attention to your thoughts and emotions. Allow yourself to observe your thoughts without judgment or attachment, and reflect on what they might be trying to tell you. With regular practice, reflective meditation can become a powerful tool for promoting happiness and well-being.

A meditation for you

Find a quiet place where you can sit or lie down comfortably. Close your eyes and take a few deep breaths, allowing yourself to relax.

Begin by reflecting on your day or a particular event that happened recently. Allow yourself to recall the details of what happened, noticing any thoughts or emotions that come up.

As you reflect on the event, try to observe it without judgment. Simply notice what happened and how it made you feel.

Now, shift your focus to your internal experience. What thoughts and emotions were present during the event? Were there any physical sensations in your body?

Take a moment to acknowledge these thoughts, emotions, and sensations without trying to change them. Simply observe them with curiosity and compassion.

Next, ask yourself what you learned from this experience. Was there a lesson or insight that emerged for you? How might you apply this insight in your life moving forward?

Finally, offer yourself some words of kindness and support. You might say something like, "May I be kind to myself in this moment" or "May I remember that I am doing the best I can."

When you feel ready, slowly open your eyes and take a few deep breaths. Allow yourself to come back to the present moment, feeling grounded and centered.

You can find the recorded version of this meditation on this page:
www.creativestartupacademy.com/resources-hf

Internal weather

The exercise "How is your internal weather?" is a **mindfulness practice** that can help you become more aware of your current emotional state. The idea behind the exercise is that just like the weather outside, our **internal emotional** state can also change from day to day, and even from moment to moment.

To do the exercise, start by finding a quiet and comfortable place to sit or lie down. Take a few deep breaths to help you relax and become more present in the moment. Then, bring your attention to your internal experience, and ask yourself the following questions:

What emotions am I feeling right now?

How intense are these emotions?

Where do I feel these emotions in my body?

How are these emotions affecting my thoughts and behaviors?

As you answer these questions, try to simply observe your emotions without judging or trying to change them. Notice any physical sensations that arise in your body, and try to stay with the present moment experience as much as possible.

By regularly practicing this exercise, you can become more aware of your internal weather and develop greater emotional intelligence. This can help you to respond more skillfully to difficult emotions and cultivate more positive emotions in your daily life.

7/11 breathing

7/11 breathing is a breathing technique that involves **breathing in for a count of 7 and breathing out for a count of 11.** This type of breathing can help to **calm** the mind and body, **reduce stress and anxiety**, and promote feelings of relaxation and happiness.

The reason this type of breathing can help with happiness is because it **activates the parasympathetic nervous system,** which is responsible for the body's rest and relaxation response. When we are stressed or anxious, the sympathetic nervous system is activated, which can lead to feelings of tension and unease.

By engaging the parasympathetic nervous system through deep breathing, we can counteract the effects of stress and promote feelings of calm and contentment.

In addition to its physiological benefits, 7/11 breathing can also help with **mindfulness and present moment awareness.**

By focusing on the sensation of the breath and counting the inhales and exhales, we can train our minds to be more attentive and present. This can help us to cultivate a greater sense of gratitude and appreciation for the present moment, which can contribute to overall feelings of happiness and well-being.

To practice 7/11 breathing, find a comfortable seated position and take a few deep breaths to center yourself. Then, breathe in deeply for a count of 7, allowing your belly to expand as you inhale. Hold the breath for a brief moment, then exhale slowly for a count of 11, allowing your belly to contract as you exhale. Repeat this cycle several times, focusing on the sensation of the breath and allowing yourself to become more relaxed and centered with each inhale and exhale.

You can find the recorded version of this meditation on this page:
www.creativestartupacademy.com/resources-hf

3 min breathing space

The 3-Minute Breathing Space is a **mindfulness exercise** that helps individuals to **ground** themselves in the present moment, **calm** their minds, and reduce stress and anxiety. It is a simple exercise that can be done anywhere, anytime, and only takes a few minutes to complete.

The exercise involves three steps:

Awareness - Start by bringing your attention to your present moment experience, noticing any thoughts, feelings, or physical sensations that are present.

Gathering - Focus your attention on your breath, noticing the sensations of breathing as you inhale and exhale. Let go of any distractions and bring your full attention to the breath.

Expanding - Expand your awareness to include your whole body, noticing any areas of tension, discomfort, or relaxation. Notice the sensations in your body as you continue to breathe.

This exercise can be done at any time during the day, whenever you feel the need to take a break from the busyness of life and connect with the present moment. By taking a few minutes to pause and focus on the breath, you can reduce stress and improve your overall sense of well-being.

Research has shown that regular mindfulness practice, including the 3-Minute Breathing Space, can help to increase positive emotions, reduce symptoms of anxiety and depression, and improve overall mental health and well-being.

You can find the recorded version of this meditation on this page:
www.creativestartupacademy.com/resources-hf

Mindfulness of breath exercise

The mindfulness of breath exercise is a simple meditation practice that involves **focusing on the sensations of breathing** to cultivate mindfulness and relaxation. Here are the steps for the mindfulness of breath exercise:

Find a quiet and comfortable place where you can sit or lie down without being disturbed.

Close your eyes or keep them softly focused on a point in front of you.

Take a few deep breaths to relax your body and calm your mind.

Bring your attention to the sensation of your breath as it flows in and out of your nose or mouth.

Notice the sensation of the air moving in and out of your body. Focus on the physical sensations of the breath, such as the feeling of coolness as you inhale and warmth as you exhale.

If your mind wanders, simply acknowledge the thought or feeling and then gently bring your attention back to the breath.

Continue to focus on your breath for several minutes or as long as you wish.
When you're ready to end the exercise, take a few deep breaths and bring your attention back to your surroundings.

Practicing mindfulness of breath regularly can help you develop a greater sense of awareness and calmness, reduce stress and anxiety, and improve your overall well-being.

You can find the recorded version of this meditation on this page:
www.creativestartupacademy.com/resources-hf

Mindful movement

Mindful movement is a form of mindfulness practice that involves **paying attention to the sensations and movements of the body as we move.** It can be a great way to cultivate awareness and connect with the present moment, as well as improve physical health and well-being.

Some examples of mindful movement practices include **yoga, tai chi, walking meditation, and qigong.** These practices can help us to tune into the present moment, let go of distractions and worries, and find a sense of calm and relaxation.

During mindful movement, we focus our attention on the physical sensations of the body as we move.

For example, during a yoga practice, we might focus on the stretch of our muscles, the rhythm of our breath, and the feeling of our feet on the ground.

By staying present in the moment and focusing our attention on these sensations, we can cultivate a sense of mindfulness and presence that can help to reduce stress and increase well-being.

In addition to improving physical health and well-being, mindful movement can also have a positive impact on mental health. Research has shown that practicing yoga, for example, can reduce symptoms of depression, anxiety, and stress, and improve overall mood and well-being.

Overall, mindful movement can be a powerful tool for cultivating mindfulness, reducing stress, and improving physical and mental health.

You can find some stretches and yoga exercises meditation on this page:
www.creativestartupacademy.com/resources-hf

Mindful body scan

A mindful body scan is a type of meditation that **involves bringing attention to different parts of your body and noticing physical sensations**, thoughts, and emotions that arise. It is a powerful tool for promoting relaxation, reducing stress and anxiety, and increasing body awareness.

Here is a mindful body scan meditation for you:
To do a mindful body scan meditation, find a comfortable position lying down on your back, with your arms by your sides and your legs uncrossed. Close your eyes and take a few deep breaths, focusing on the sensation of the air moving in and out of your body.

Start by bringing your attention to your feet. Notice any sensations that arise in this part of your body, such as warmth, tingling, or tension. Try to just observe the sensations without judgment or analysis.

Slowly move your attention up through your body, focusing on each body part in turn. Spend a few moments on each part of your body, noticing any physical sensations or tension you may feel. If you notice any areas of tension or discomfort, try to soften or relax those areas with your breath.

As you move through your body, notice any thoughts or emotions that arise, but try not to get caught up in them. Instead, acknowledge them and gently bring your attention back to the physical sensations in your body.

Once you have scanned your entire body, take a few deep breaths and notice how you feel. You may feel more relaxed, centered, and aware of your body than before you started. You can practice this exercise for as long or as short as you like, depending on your needs and schedule. Even just a few minutes of mindful body scanning can be helpful in promoting relaxation and reducing stress.

You can find the recorded version of this meditation on this page:
www.creativestartupacademy.com/resources-hf

Daily mindfulness club

Bestselling author Shamash Alidina has created a daily mindfulness club in which you can meet daily with other people for meditations and connecting
https://dailymindfulnessclub.com

Loving kindness meditation

Loving-kindness meditation, also known as **Metta meditation,** is a type of meditation practice that cultivates feelings of love, **kindness, and compassion towards oneself and others**. The practice involves repeating specific phrases or mantras to generate positive emotions and foster a sense of connectedness with others.

Here is a meditation for you:
To begin a loving-kindness meditation practice, find a quiet and comfortable place to sit or lie down. Close your eyes and take a few deep breaths to relax your body and mind. Then, focus on generating feelings of love and kindness towards yourself by repeating the following phrases silently or out loud:

May I be happy
May I be healthy
May I be safe
May I live with ease

Visualize yourself surrounded by warm, loving energy and feel the positive emotions flowing through your body. When you feel ready, expand your focus to include others, starting with someone you love and care for deeply. Repeat the same phrases towards this person, visualizing them surrounded by love and positive energy.

May you be happy
May you be healthy
May you be safe
May you live with ease

Next, gradually extend these feelings to include people who are neutral to you, such as strangers or acquaintances. Repeat the same phrases towards them, visualizing them surrounded by love and positive energy.

Repeat the following phrases silently or out loud:

May you be happy
May you be healthy
May you be safe
May you live with ease

Finally, extend your feelings of love and kindness to all beings, including those who may have caused you harm or difficulty in the past. Repeat the same phrases towards them, visualizing them surrounded by love and positive energy.

May we be happy
May we be healthy
May we be safe
May we live with ease

Finish the practice by taking a few deep breaths and noticing how you feel. Practicing loving-kindness meditation regularly can help increase positive emotions, reduce negative emotions, and foster a greater sense of connection and compassion towards oneself and others.

You can find the recorded version of this meditation on this page:
www.creativestartupacademy.com/resources-hf

Everyday mindfulness activities

Welcome to this chapter on **daily mindful activities and their relationship with happiness**. Mindfulness is the practice of **being present and fully engaged in the present moment, without judgment or distraction**. Research has shown that practicing mindfulness can have a positive impact on our overall well-being, including increased happiness and reduced stress. In this chapter, we will explore various daily mindful activities that you can incorporate into your routine to enhance your happiness and well-being. From meditation and breathing exercises to mindful eating and gratitude practices, we will delve into the benefits of each activity and provide practical tips on how to incorporate them into your daily life. So, let's dive in and discover the power of daily mindfulness for cultivating happiness!

Mindful Breathing

Take a few minutes each day to focus on your breath. Close your eyes and take deep, slow breaths, feeling the sensation of the air moving in and out of your body.

Mindful Eating

Pay attention to your food while you eat. Take time to savor each bite, and notice the texture, taste, and smell of your food.

Mindful Walking

Take a walk and pay attention to your surroundings. Notice the sounds, smells, and sensations around you as you move.

Gratitude Journaling

Each day, write down a few things that you are grateful for. This can help you focus on the positive aspects of your life and increase feelings of happiness and contentment.
Remember to download your gratitude journal here:
www.creativestartupacademy.com/resources-hf

Mindful Listening

Practice active listening by really focusing on what someone is saying without interrupting or thinking about your response.

Mindful Stretching

Take a few minutes to stretch your body, paying attention to the sensations in your muscles and joints as you move.

Mindful Showering

Pay attention to the sensation of the water on your skin, the smell of the soap, and the temperature of the water while taking a shower.

Mindful Cleaning

Focus on the act of cleaning, whether it's washing dishes or sweeping the floor. Notice the physical sensations and movements involved in the task.

Mindful Breathing

Mindful Breathing during mundane activities: take deep, slow breaths while doing something mundane like waiting in line or doing the dishes.

Mindful bedtime routine

Create a calming bedtime routine that includes practices such as gentle stretching, deep breathing, reading a book, or meditation to help you relax and prepare for sleep.

Self compassion meditation

Self-compassion meditation is a practice that involves **cultivating a kind, accepting, and non-judgmental attitude towards oneself.** It can be a powerful tool for reducing self-criticism, promoting self-acceptance, and improving emotional well-being. Self-compassion meditation typically involves **three key elements: mindfulness, self-kindness, and common humanity.**

Here is an example of a self-compassion meditation:
Find a comfortable and quiet place where you can sit or lie down undisturbed for a few minutes.

Take a few deep breaths and allow yourself to relax.

Begin by bringing to mind a difficult situation or challenge that you have experienced recently.

Notice any negative thoughts or feelings that arise, but try not to judge them. Simply observe them with curiosity and compassion.

Now, bring your attention to your body. Notice any areas of tension or discomfort and imagine sending kindness and warmth to those parts of your body.

Next, repeat to yourself some compassionate phrases or mantras that resonate with you, such as "may I be kind to myself," "may I accept myself just as I am," or "may I find peace and healing." Repeat these phrases several times, allowing yourself to fully embody the intention of each one.

Finally, bring to mind a sense of common humanity by acknowledging that everyone experiences difficulties and challenges in life. Recognize that you are not alone in your struggles and that you deserve compassion and understanding just like anyone else.

When you are ready, take a few deep breaths and slowly open your eyes, returning to the present moment with a greater sense of compassion and self-acceptance.

By practicing self-compassion meditation regularly, you can develop greater resilience, emotional well-being, and a more positive relationship with yourself.

You can find the recorded version of this meditation on this page:
www.creativestartupacademy.com/resources-hf

Self compassion letter

Writing a self-compassion letter can be a **powerful tool for cultivating self-love and self-acceptance**. Here's a guide on how to write one:

Part One

Write about which imperfections make you feel inadequate

Take some time to reflect on which imperfections or flaws make you feel inadequate or insecure. These could be things like:

Physical appearance (e.g. weight, height, skin, etc.)

Personality traits (e.g. shyness, lack of confidence, tendency to be critical, etc.)

Mistakes or failures (e.g. a past relationship, a job loss, an academic setback, etc.)

Life circumstances (e.g. financial struggles, family issues, health challenges, etc.)

Write down these imperfections or flaws in a list or a paragraph. Don't judge yourself for having them or feel ashamed about them. Instead, acknowledge them with kindness and curiosity, like you would with a good friend.

Part Two

Letter: Write a letter to yourself from the perspective of an unconditionally loving imaginary friend

Now, imagine that you have an unconditionally loving imaginary friend who knows all about your imperfections and loves you just the same. This friend sees you with compassion and understanding, and wants to offer you comfort and support.

Write a letter to yourself from this perspective. Start with a greeting like "Dear [Your Name]," and then write as if you were speaking directly to yourself. Use kind, gentle language that reflects the unconditional love and acceptance of your imaginary friend.

In the letter, you could include:

Acknowledgment of your imperfections: Start by acknowledging the imperfections or flaws you listed earlier. Let yourself know that it's okay to have these imperfections and that they don't make you any less worthy of love and respect.

Validation of your feelings: Validate any emotions or feelings you have about your imperfections. Let yourself know that it's normal to feel insecure, anxious, or ashamed about them, and that these feelings are valid and understandable.

Compassion and understanding: Offer yourself compassion and understanding for your imperfections. Use phrases like "I'm sorry you're going through this," "I understand how hard this must be for you," or "I'm here for you no matter what."

Encouragement and support: Offer yourself encouragement and support for dealing with your imperfections. Use phrases like "I believe in you," "You're doing the best you can," or "I know you'll get through this." Remind yourself of your strengths, resilience, and inner resources.

Unconditional love: End the letter with expressions of unconditional love and acceptance. Use phrases like "I love you just the way you are," "You're perfect in your imperfections," or "You're worthy of love and respect no matter what."

Part Three

Feel the compassion as it soothes you

After you finish writing the letter, take some time to read it over and let the words sink in. Imagine that your imaginary friend is speaking directly to you with love and compassion.

Notice how you feel as you read the letter. Do you feel a sense of relief, comfort, or warmth? Do you feel more self-acceptance and self-love? Allow yourself to feel these emotions and let them soothe you.

You could also try reading the letter out loud or recording yourself reading it and listening to it later. Repeat this exercise as often as you need, and feel free to modify or add to the letter as you go along. Remember, self-compassion is a skill that takes practice, so be patient and gentle with yourself as you learn.

Write a letter here:

Gratitude meditation

Gratitude is the quality of being **thankful and showing appreciation** for what one has in life. It is a powerful tool that can help rewire our brains and lead to greater happiness and well-being. By focusing on the good in our lives, we can shift our mindset to one of abundance and positivity.

Gratitude meditation is a practice that involves intentionally focusing on the things we are grateful for in life. This could be anything from our health, our loved ones, our homes, our careers, or even the simple pleasures in life like a beautiful sunset or a warm cup of tea. By taking time to reflect on these things, we can cultivate a deeper sense of gratitude and appreciation for all that we have.

The benefits of gratitude are numerous. Studies have shown that practicing gratitude can lead to greater **happiness**, **improved relationships**, **better physical health**, and even **a stronger immune system**. It can also reduce stress, anxiety, and depression by shifting our focus away from negative thoughts and emotions.

Gratitude also has the power to **rewire our brains**. By regularly practicing gratitude, we can create new neural pathways in the brain that reinforce positive thinking and emotions. This can lead to a more optimistic outlook on life and an increased ability to cope with difficult situations.

Overall, gratitude is a simple yet powerful tool that can have a profound impact on our lives. Whether through meditation or simply taking time each day to reflect on the things we are grateful for, cultivating a spirit of gratitude can help us find greater joy, contentment, and fulfillment in life.

Here's a simple gratitude meditation:

Find a quiet and comfortable place where you can sit or lie down without being disturbed.

Take a few deep breaths and focus on your breath, letting your body relax and release any tension.

Begin to bring to mind the things in your life that you are grateful for, both big and small.

Take some time to really feel gratitude for each of these things, allowing the positive emotions to fill your body and mind.

As you focus on each thing you are grateful for, repeat a simple phrase to yourself, such as "Thank you" or "I am grateful for..."

Continue to repeat these phrases and focus on your feelings of gratitude for as long as you like, allowing the positive emotions to grow and expand.

When you are ready, take a few more deep breaths and slowly open your eyes, bringing your gratitude with you as you go about your day.

Remember, gratitude is a powerful tool for rewiring your brain and improving your overall happiness and well-being. By regularly practicing gratitude, you can train your brain to focus on the positive and cultivate a more positive outlook on life.

You can find the recorded version of this meditation on this page:
www.creativestartupacademy.com/resources-hf

Goal visualization

Goal visualization is a technique **that involves imagining oneself achieving a specific goal**. It is based on the idea that mental imagery can help prepare the mind and body for actual performance, and can **increase motivation and confidence**.

When we visualize ourselves achieving our goals, it creates a sense of **excitement** and **motivation** within us. It also helps us to clarify our goals and **create a plan** of **action** towards achieving them.

Here is an exercise for goal visualization:

Choose a specific goal that you would like to achieve. It could be a personal or professional goal.

Find a quiet and comfortable place where you can sit or lie down and relax.

Close your eyes and take a few deep breaths to relax your mind and body.

Visualize yourself achieving your goal in great detail. Imagine yourself in the moment, how you feel, what you see and hear. Imagine the positive outcomes and how achieving this goal will contribute to your overall happiness and well-being.

Focus on the process of achieving the goal, including the specific actions you need to take to make it happen. See yourself taking those actions and succeeding in each step.

Repeat this exercise regularly, ideally daily or a few times a week. Keep your goal in mind and take action towards it every day.

Goal visualization can be a powerful tool for increasing happiness and motivation. By focusing on the positive outcomes and taking action towards our goals, we can create a sense of purpose and accomplishment in our lives.

Mental contrasting

Mental contrasting is a technique used to help individuals **achieve their goals by visualizing their desired future outcomes** while also considering **potential obstacles** that may arise. The idea behind this technique is to help people overcome the potential barriers that may prevent them from achieving their goals and ultimately increase their happiness and well-being.

The technique involves **two steps**: first, individuals are asked to **visualize** their **desired** future **outcomes** in vivid detail. This includes imagining what it will feel like to achieve their goal, what it will look like, and what they will be doing once they have achieved it. This step is intended to create a positive and motivating vision for the future.

The second step involves **considering potential obstacles** or barriers that **may prevent them** from achieving their goals. This step is intended to help individuals identify and prepare for potential challenges that may arise, such as time constraints, lack of resources, or competing priorities. By considering these obstacles in advance, individuals are better equipped to overcome them and remain motivated towards achieving their goals.

Research has shown that mental contrasting can be an effective tool for **increasing motivation** and goal attainment. Studies have found that individuals who engage in mental contrasting are more likely to take action towards achieving their goals and are more successful in achieving them compared to those who only visualize their desired outcomes without considering potential obstacles.

To practice mental contrasting, you can follow these steps:

Identify a specific goal that you want to achieve. Visualize your desired outcome in vivid detail, imagining what it will feel like to achieve your goal.

Consider potential obstacles or challenges that may arise and visualize how you will overcome them.

Repeat this exercise regularly to keep yourself motivated and focused on achieving your goal.

By practicing mental contrasting, you can increase your motivation and likelihood of achieving your goals, ultimately leading to increased happiness and well-being.

Research has shown that the **mental contrasting effect can last for up to 24 months.** In a study published in the Journal of Experimental Social Psychology, participants who engaged in mental contrasting for their goals had significantly higher goal attainment rates compared to those who only engaged in positive thinking or did not engage in any goal-related thinking at all. The effect was also found to persist for up to two years after the initial mental contrasting exercise.

This suggests that mental contrasting can be a powerful tool for goal achievement and long-term happiness. By identifying potential obstacles and planning for them, individuals are better equipped to navigate challenges and stay on track towards their desired outcomes.

Friday pulse

Friday Pulse is a company founded by **Nic Marks**, a well-known expert in happiness and well-being at work. The company focuses on measuring and improving employee engagement, well-being, and happiness in the workplace. Friday Pulse uses a **weekly survey system** that measures employees' happiness and engagement levels, providing actionable insights to organizations to improve their work culture. By measuring employee well-being and engagement, organizations can identify potential issues and take action to create a more positive work environment. The ultimate goal of Friday Pulse is to help organizations build happier and more productive workplaces where employees can thrive. You might want to consider the product in your company.

Via character strengths survey

The **VIA Character Strengths Survey** is a **psychological assessment** tool designed to help individuals identify their **core character strengths**. Developed by **Christopher Peterson and Martin Seligman**, the survey is based on the research findings of positive psychology, which focuses on identifying the strengths that enable individuals to thrive and lead fulfilling lives.

The VIA survey consists of a set of **24 character strengths,** which are grouped under six core virtues: wisdom, courage, humanity, justice, temperance, and transcendence. These strengths include traits such as creativity, curiosity, kindness, fairness, self-control, and spirituality, among others.

The survey is designed to provide individuals with a better understanding of their own character strengths, and to help them identify areas in which they may wish to further develop themselves. By recognizing and developing their core strengths, individuals are better equipped to cope with life's challenges, build positive relationships, and find meaning and purpose in their lives.

The VIA survey has been widely used in a variety of settings, including schools, workplaces, and mental health clinics. It has been found to be a useful tool for promoting personal growth and well-being, as well as for enhancing interpersonal communication and collaboration.

While the VIA survey does not provide a complete picture of an individual's personality or character, it can serve as a helpful starting point for self-discovery and personal development.

You can take your survey here:
https://www.viacharacter.org/survey/account/register

A final word

Congratulations on finishing "The Happiness Formula" book! You have now gained valuable knowledge and tools that you can implement in your life to improve your overall happiness and well-being. It is important to remember that change takes time, and it is okay to take things step by step. Do not feel overwhelmed by the amount of information provided in the book. Instead, take your time to reflect on what you have learned and focus on implementing one or two changes at a time. Remember that happiness is a journey, not a destination, and that you have the power to make positive changes in your life. Thank you for reading, and I wish you all the best on your happiness journey.

About Christine

Christine, a Berlin native, spent 7 years working as a Strategic Consultant & Senior Account Manager in marketing & design agencies before she decided it was time for a change in 2009.

She left her job and embarked on a three-month journey through New Zealand & Australia before settling in London the following year. Initially, Christine worked as a Senior Account Manager in a new agency, but she soon realized that it wasn't the right fit for her. Seeking greater fulfillment, she pursued training as a Coach and obtained a certificate in Neuro Linguistic Programming (NLP).

Christine became known as the Marketing and Creative Start-Up Coach, dedicated to helping others find happiness in their professional pursuits.

Over the years, Christine has worked with universities to help students launch their own businesses, as well as with individuals and small businesses seeking guidance with marketing and entrepreneurship. Through her Creative Start-Up Academy, she provides a range of resources to help entrepreneurs succeed.

Beyond her professional pursuits, Christine is an avid painter, knitter, and ukulele player, finding joy and creativity through these outlets. She prioritizes self-care through mindfulness, meditation, and exercise, and cherishes time spent with both loved ones and on solo adventures. Find out more www.creativestartupacademy.com

Your review

Thank you for choosing to read 'The Happiness Formula'! I hope that you found the book informative and inspiring, and that it has helped you to cultivate greater happiness and well-being in your life. If you enjoyed the book, I would be extremely grateful if you could take a few moments to leave a review on Amazon. Reviews are a crucial part of helping new readers discover the book and are greatly appreciated. Thank you again for your support, and we wish you continued happiness and fulfillment!

Notes

Notes

Notes

Notes

Notes

Printed in Great Britain
by Amazon

25903585R00155